Hua, Julietta.
Trafficking
women's human rights

Trafficking Women's Human Rights

Julietta Hua

University of Minnesota Press | Minneapolis | London

The University of Minnesota Press gratefully acknowledges financial assistance provided for the publication of this book from the Office of Faculty Affairs and the College of Humanities, San Francisco State University.

A version of chapter 2 was published previously as Julietta Hua and Holly Nigorizawa, "Sex Trafficking, Women's Rights, and the Politics of Representation," *International Feminist Journal of Politics,* Special Issue: New Directions in Feminism and Human Rights 24, no. 4 (2010), www.informaworld.com.

Published by the University of Minnesota Press
111 Third Avenue South, Suite 290
Minneapolis, MN 55401–2520
http://www.upress.umn.edu

Library of Congress Cataloging-in-Publication Data

Hua, Julietta.
    Trafficking women's human rights / Julietta Hua.
        p. cm.
    Includes bibliographical references and index.
    ISBN 978-0-8166-7560-9 (hc : alk. paper)
    ISBN 978-0-8166-7561-6 (pb : alk. paper)
    1. Human trafficking. 2. Human rights. 3. Women's rights.
4. Women—Legal status, laws, etc. 5. Feminism. I. Title.
    HQ281.H82 2011
    323.3'2949—dc23

                                    2011016428

Printed in the United States of America on acid-free paper

The University of Minnesota is an equal-opportunity educator and employer.

18 17 16 15 14 13 12 11   10 9 8 7 6 5 4 3 2 1

Contents

Preface

The police protect; the police terrorize. NGOs provide important services to people who need them; NGOs reproduce inequalities and hierarchies. Laws like the Victims of Trafficking and Violence Protection Act (VTVPA), which actualize human rights, extend aid and help to positively alter life circumstances; laws like the VTVPA do not aid but further criminalize immigrants. These seemingly oppositional either–or statements capture the different perspectives from which to understand social relations; the police either protect or they terrorize.

For my students, whose optimism and perpetual dedication to fighting to make the world a better place continue to humble me, finding the causes of injustice is a key aspect to strategizing change. Thus in the classroom we often discuss whether laws, social services, and NGOs work in negative or positive ways: Are they helping or hurting? Are they the cause of injustice or are they the remedy? From my colleagues who teach literature and visual culture classes, I have learned that the desire to locate positive and negative representations is also often the first instinct in analyzing art, film, novels, and so on. Part of this instinctive desire to frame understandings of social and cultural artifacts as either positive or negative comes from both the ideological tools readily available to us—like those anchored in capitalism that privilege seeing the world through cost-benefit analyses—and from the relative ease that comes with a framework that provides clear-cut choices, either–or choices that allow us to situate ourselves on one side or another. After all, solutions are easier to locate when we have a clearer sense of how social issues have negative or positive impacts.

What I hope this book will do is challenge the privileging of the either–or framework. I want to move away from simply quantifying and qualifying through positive and negative terms to resituating analysis to focus on how we come to privilege certain lenses and frameworks.

For example, NGOs both provide important resources that fundamentally make lives better even as they also reproduce and further embed structural inequalities. As the seven women members of the organization Sangtin eloquently demonstrate in their collaborative writing *Playing with Fire,* the same NGO that helped bring food, water, and other resources to Uttar Pradesh, India, and that helped Sangtin meet to "envision and rebuild [its] interconnected worlds," also reproduced social inequalities within the NGO hierarchy and attempted to silence and own the work of the collective.[1] The works of the Sangtin Collective and Richa Nagar, the INCITE! collective, Deborah Mindry, Nancy Naples, and Manisha Desai, among many others, crystallize the ways NGOs are neither good nor bad institutions. Rather, they are complex, contradictory mechanisms that help shape our understanding of the world around us. These authors remind us that the important point to consider is not whether the impact of NGOs is positive or negative, but how the contradictions embedded in NGO-ization (the "processes by which development ideology is reproduced in the resistant spaces of political action")[2] point to the complex and multiple ways power works to shape social realities—both the social realities that oppress and that empower.

By using human rights, many people around the world have found a strong justification for advocating improved living conditions (for instance, in Bolivia, where people have organized to maintain public access to water by using human rights as a means to frame the significance of this move). Yet the mobilization of human rights arguments also justifies neocolonial and uneven global relationships, for instance, by deploying "the concept of 'third world' non-European 'backwardness' to explain why the 'third world' lacks human rights," as Inderpal Grewal articulates.[3] Human rights help and hinder; human rights are defined through top-down mechanisms even as they are also shaped through localized actions. This is the premise where the book begins as it endeavors to understand the multiple and varied mechanisms of power and knowledge at work in shaping the reality of antitrafficking efforts—efforts that provide invaluable recognition and aid even as they might also inflict their own forms of violence.

The questions that drive this book also come out of personal frustrations with the ways feminist and antiracist language, arguments, and actions are often also enabling antifeminist and racist ends. For example, the legislative decision for affirmative-action programs to help address the historical embedding of structural inequalities, while imperfect, nonetheless attempted to reorganize social relations in antiracist terms. Yet affirmative-action claims have also enabled outcomes like *University of California Regents v. Bakke* (1978), which used the language of equal protection to protect white privilege by striking down the University of California, Davis, medical school's special admissions program "designed to assure the admission of a specified number of students from certain minority groups," according to Justice Powell.[4] Similarly, the use of certain kinds of feminist arguments (namely, those labeled "liberal feminisms") to justify war in Afghanistan and Iraq after 9/11 made strange bedfellows of politically radical feminist organizations and politically conservative government entities. These examples are often described as moments of appropriation; I see them also as symptoms of something else. Thus this project is also driven by a desire to understand how such appropriations are made possible—of what are these moments of appropriation symptoms? There is something in the way that we frame arguments and the way we see situations that allows for the appropriation of feminist and antiracist language for ends that neither support feminist or antiracist goals. The many political and intellectual arguments and actions we call feminism are more complex than simply being either antipatriarchal or not. Feminisms are both emancipatory and they are not. How discourses of feminism have been shaped and defined, how they have been conceptualized and thought out, have everything to do with why feminist frameworks can be both emancipatory and also repressive.

It is certainly less complicated to see things through an either–or lens, especially when it comes to human rights. However, when we re-shift the lens so that the questions are posed differently, we can begin to see the myriad complex ways structural and discursive mechanisms work to help shape our understandings of the world around us. I believe this is a necessary and important intellectual exercise, even at the risk of seeming too abstract or ungrounded. The intellectual and conceptual exercise of understanding how we come to see and know something as such is important because the conceptual conditions tied to how we know a thing are directly tied to our understandings of (and therefore ability to alter) what we call the material, or real. As M. Jacqui Alexander and Chandra Mohanty note, "We literally have to think ourselves out of these crises through collective praxis and particular kinds of theorizing."[5] How we come to know a thing is thus crucial to the so-called material reality of that thing. In other words, addressing the materiality of human rights violations, poverty and inequality, gender-based violence, and so on is at the heart of this work, but this materiality is shaped into particular forms through discursive mechanisms that help us see and know a thing one way and not another. It is from these premises that the book begins my effort to try to show how the more abstract, conceptual conditions very much shape the so-called real aspects of human rights and gendered violence.

Acknowledgments

The University of Minnesota, Humphrey Institute of Public Affairs, Program for the Study of Race, Gender, and Public Policy provided an academic year of support to enable writing and publication. Samuel Myers Jr. and Sally Kenney, as program cofounders and directors, and Sudha Shetty were especially generous with their professional guidance an d mentorship. My fellow comrades in the program, Vera Fennell and Roxanne Ornales, provided great intellectual and emotional support.

Thank you to Yen Le Espiritu, Laura Kang, Richa Nagar, David Pellow, Denise Ferreira da Silva, and Lisa Yoneyama for their continued support over the years, and Pieter Martin and Kristian Tvedten at the University of Minnesota Press. Lisa Park provided especially generative and inspirational feedback; most of what is good about the book is thanks to her and the other anonymous reviewer. I especially thank Neda Atanasoski and Grace Kim for many years of talking with me about the broader issues behind the book and for reading drafts.

My colleagues in Women and Gender Studies at San Francisco State University, Nan Boyd, Deb Cohler, AJ Jaimes Guerrero, Kasturi Ray, Jillian Sandell, and Lisa Tresca, as well as the exceptional dean of the college, Paul Sherwin, have provided a wonderful working environment, without which the book would never have been finished. The president's office at SFSU also provided a semester of paid leave, which enabled me to focus on writing. At SFSU, I met and briefly employed the best research assistant I could never have imagined, Holly Nigorizawa, whose long hours tracking down trafficking prosecution case files made possible chapters 2 and 3, much of which is reprinted from our coauthored article for *International Feminist Journal of Politics*.

Introduction:
The Legal Stakes of Human Trafficking

WHAT IS AT STAKE in understanding certain issues as human rights concerns and not others? How, why, and to what effect does the defining of women's human rights through the stories and images of Latin American, African, and Asian women—"other" women in other places—have on the idea of human rights and the project of feminism? What is the legacy of the modern epistemologies informing notions of rights, humanity, and the law? In what ways do they continue to shape contemporary discussions of human rights? This book investigates why certain forms of violence come to be defined as human rights violations while others do not. Examining how dominant definitions and meanings come to be attached to the terms of human rights is an important exercise because "creating a name for a problem is one of those subtle cultural technologies that defines an issue and channels responses to it."[1]

The question of who counts as human has as contested a history as the question of what counts as rights. Philosophers, scientists, clergy, and politicians alike have struggled to answer whether there is a universal definition that can capture the essence of humanity and whether making claim to the category ensures a set of entitlements that can be recognized and respected across linguistic, historical, national, and cultural difference. These difficulties continue to shape contemporary human rights discourses, where both critics and advocates of human rights flag the universalizing tendencies that can sometimes privilege so-called Western agendas and lenses in human rights talk. *Trafficking Women's Human Rights* traces the intellectual and philosophical origins of the concept of human rights and asks to what extent human rights can serve as a productive site to address global gender violence given this tendency to sometimes universalize so-called Western priorities. Looking specifically at the ways sex trafficking has been legally and culturally shaped as a human rights violation in the United States, this book traces the ways human rights works as a modern epistemology or body of knowledge. Understanding how sex trafficking is represented in mainstream U.S. discourses as a women's human rights issue also reveals how meanings around national belonging are implicitly conveyed through campaigns to address human rights violations assumed to take place elsewhere.

How we come to define human rights speaks volumes about the values and perspectives privileged in human rights talk as well as demonstrates how efforts to address human rights are already prescribed by the ways we see and define the problem and its subjects. This book has four main aims: first, understanding the discursive processes through which we come to know a thing as a human right or a human rights violation; second, understanding the ontological conditions—conditions tied to being—through which humanity constitutes, circumscribes, and confers subjectivity; third, demonstrating how taking for granted the ontological conditions tied to humanity reproduces the uneven configurations of power that once informed the period of European empire building and the transatlantic slave trade; and fourth, illustrating how our understandings of human rights and the global are intimately connected to domestic discourses of race relations and national belonging.

These aims are explored through a look at the rise of sex trafficking as a global and national human rights issue in the late 1990s and into the 2000s. Sex trafficking offers a unique site for engaging in the more abstract questions around how to define rights and humanity for several reasons. As a human rights violation, trafficking has a clear origin in terms of when it became a documented, legislated human rights concern for both the United States and the United Nations (2000). This does not mean that the activities now defined as trafficking did not exist before its political and legislative birth; rather, trafficking activities were named such, criminalized, and institutionalized into the formal legal structures of the United States at a specific moment. Having this moment of origin makes it more straightforward in some ways to trace how state, NGO, media, and academic players worked together to delineate what activities would count as trafficking and what it would take to claim victimization. Second, defining trafficked subjects through lenses that posit victimization against agency (coercion against choice) makes sex trafficking a particularly rich site where the conditionality of human rights can be explored. One of the arguments this book makes is about the conditional nature of claiming rights, tied in large part to the modern and liberal principles taken for granted in much of the talk around human rights. These assumed and naturalized values and frameworks work to constrict the ways victimhood can be imagined; for instance, sex trafficking victims must be distinguishable from illegal aliens or prostitutes, whose assumed consent writes them as criminals and not victims. Finally, the way trafficking has been compared to eighteenth- and nineteenth-century activities of transatlantic slavery makes it a unique site where international discourses of human rights are informed by and help inform U.S. national discourses of race relations.

Although there is a strong body of literature aimed at describing trafficking activities based on ethnographic research—for instance, Laura Maria Agustin's work on global sex work—the goal of this book is slightly different. It looks at how human trafficking has been talked about in media, in research, by the state, and by nongovernmental organizations to understand how the making of sex trafficking into a human rights concern reveals the racial, gendered, and sexual discourses at work in shaping a national sense of identity and belonging. Rather than focus on the question, What is trafficking? this book asks, How does trafficking get talked about? How do the ways we talk about trafficking speak to broader questions about the limits of human rights and the racialized and gendered processes of policing national belonging? The book is interested in making visible the process through which certain activities become understood and included under the category and label of trafficking, and in making visible the impact of such processes on how national and human rights subjectivity is imagined. Working from the criticisms and insights authored by a small body of feminist scholars interested in sex trafficking and prostitution (Laura Maria Agustin, Beverly Balos, Wendy Chapkis, Julia O'Connell Davidson, Jo Doezema, Kamala Kempadoo, Gretchen Soderlund, Kay Warren), the book situates trafficking within the broader scope of discursive production and meaning-making around human rights projects.

How we have come to understand sex trafficking as a human rights violation, specifically one that enacts gendered violence and imagines victimhood in particular ways, points to the ontological conditions—the conditions through which *being* is imagined and conferred—

circumscribing the concept of human rights. While calls to humanity and human rights are envisioned as the ultimate form of establishing freedom and universalism, *humanity* and *human* are vexed terms produced through a constitutive negation in the conceptual and ontological formation of modern knowledge. As Saidiya Hartman demonstrates, the conferring of humanity, though defined as that which emancipates subjects (particularly the enslaved), is in fact a more complicated process that acts also to "tether, bind and oppress."[2] Understanding the contradictions through which we define human rights and humanity is a necessary intellectual exercise if we are interested in maximizing the promise of human rights.

Human rights concerns like sex trafficking are not just about providing aid to those in need; they are also about the very ways we have come to know and understand what and who counts as human. Addressing the real violences inflicted on people who find themselves in socially vulnerable positions requires understanding the frameworks and paradigms used to understand social issues like human trafficking. This is because how responses are imagined is inevitably tied to how the problem is framed. By looking at the ways one human rights violation has been defined and made into a pressing social issue through both law and culture, this book presents the mutually constitutive ways race, gender, sexuality, and nation work to organize regimes of knowledge that then explain and naturalize uneven relationships of power. Understanding and being attentive to these underlying frames can help in shaping productive responses to migration, displacement, violence, and exploitation.

Taking to heart both the project of feminism and the concerns of what is often categorically referred to as the postcolonial critique, this book examines the production of sex trafficking discourse as a unique site where the tensions, contradictions, and convergence of human rights and identity politics in the U.S. political field are made explicit. Mapping a discourse also means creating an archive; this book thus looks to government documents including a range of congressional hearings, trafficking reports and studies; presidential addresses; transcripts from antitrafficking cases; media sources, including news media coverage, journalist narratives, and public service announcements; and nongovernmental organization literature, studies, and research. The archive also includes observations, informal interviews, and informational materials gathered at public antitrafficking conferences sponsored by local San Francisco and Minneapolis/St. Paul advocacy organizations. These conferences are funded in part through government-allocated resources established through the Victims of Trafficking and Violence Protection Act and are directed toward social service providers and concerned citizens to raise awareness of trafficking activities. The texts and archive of knowledge produced through these multiple sites help shape dominant ways of understanding trafficking and its subjects. Together, the knowledge produced through these sites constructs truths about trafficking that then work as regulatory norms. This book seeks to understand how such regimes of knowledge are actually constructed and expose how they shape reality, rather than simply explain it—a necessary and pressing task for expanding human rights as a positive tool for human betterment.

The Making of Sex Trafficking

With the passage of the Trafficking Victims Protection Act (TVPA) in 2000, human trafficking became a legal reality in the United States. Packaged with the Violence Against Women Act (HR 3355), designed in part to extend protections to battered noncitizen dependents, the Victims of Trafficking and Violence Protection Act (VTVPA; Public Law 106-386, HR 3244) explicitly made an international human rights issue (as recognized by the United Nations) into U.S. law. The law was passed to address the estimated 50,000 victims, mostly women and children,[3] who find themselves trafficked into the United States every year for various kinds of labor, including "commercial sex acts, debt bondage, and involuntary servitude."[4] Signed into law by President Bill Clinton on October 28, 2000, and sponsored by New Jersey Republican representative Christopher Smith, the law is generally recognized as a bipartisan success and has experienced little resistance in subsequent reauthorizations in 2003 (HR 2620), 2005 (HR 972), and 2008 (HR 7311). The initial law passed the Senate 90–5 (with 5 abstaining) and the House 371–1 (with 62 abstaining).[5]

The law defines the context of trafficking as one that foregrounds sexual exploitation of women and children and enumerates several specific activities into which victims are trafficked, including "prostitution, pornography, sex tourism, and other commercial sexual services."[6] The definition of trafficking adopted by the law identifies "severe forms of trafficking in persons" as follows:

A. Sex trafficking in which a commercial sex act is induced by force, fraud or coercion, or in which the person induced to perform such an act has not attained 18 years of age; or

B. The recruitment, harboring, transportation, provision, or obtaining of a person for labor or services, through the use of force, fraud, or coercion for the purposes of subjection to involuntary servitude, peonage, debt bondage, or slavery.[7]

Coercion is also specifically defined in the law as:

A. Threats of serious harm to or physical restraint against any person;

B. Any scheme, plan, or pattern intended to cause a person to believe that failure to perform an act would result in serious harm to or physical restraint against any person; or

C. The abuse or threatened abuse of the legal process.[8]

These definitions point to the severity of the activity in inflicting harm, and the law further points out that this harm is often gender based, where women, as a result of their "low status" (in the words of the law) and thus disproportionate burden of poverty in many places around the world, are more susceptible to finding themselves victims of trafficking. Hot spots for the trafficking of women in particular include, in order, Asia (particularly South and Southeast Asia), Eastern Europe and the former USSR, Africa, and Latin America. The initial version of the law focuses on the trafficking of persons across national borders, but the 2008 reauthorization stresses intrastate or domestic trafficking as another aspect of these activities.

Although the activities that are now described as trafficking have existed before being named as such, the passage of the VTVPA helped to materialize trafficking, and especially sex trafficking, as a reality. This materialization happened through various VTVPA-initiated activities, including the establishment of the Office to Monitor and Combat Trafficking chaired by the secretary of state, annual country reports issued by the Department of State that provide an assessment of trafficking worldwide, the withholding of nonhumanitarian aid for countries not meeting the minimum standards to combat trafficking, establishment of programs and initiatives abroad to assist in reintegration and resettlement of victims, money to help victims and prosecute traffickers and johns, increased penalties for traffickers, and the 2002 establishment of a special T visa for victims of trafficking. In essence, the VTVPA created an infrastructure and bureaucracy tied to addressing and combating trafficking that spans multiple government agencies.

However, as an underground activity where "all estimates are unreliable,"[9] the first hurdle for the new infrastructure was, and continues to be, materializing the nebulous, often unquantifiable problem that the bureaucracy was created to address.[10] In other words, because trafficking is defined as elusive and difficult to track according to the very documents and entities created to remedy it as a problem, the Department of State and the Office to Monitor and Combat Trafficking are under constant pressure to provide proof that the problem really does exist, that trafficking is in fact widespread, and that there are real bodies involved, however difficult they are to count and identify. Creating some sense of what trafficking is and then being able to point to specific instances of trafficking as well as specific persons who are victimized by it helps justify the millions of dollars—an estimated $375 million between 2001 and 2005[11]—allocated every year to antitrafficking efforts.

Discourse and the Policing of National Belonging

In a short statement, noting the ways language like *sex worker* used to refer to potential victims of trafficking can rationalize trafficking activities and demean victims, former ambassador and director of the Office to Monitor and Combat Trafficking John Miller gestures to an important discussion around the politics of representation and the production of knowledge:

Language is as important in fighting modern-day slavery, also known as human trafficking, as it was in fighting historic slavery. . . . People called "sex workers" did not choose prostitution the way most of us choose work occupations as pointed out by President Bush's Directive issued four years ago. . . . To abolish modern-day slavery we must not be afraid to call slavery by its real, despicable name.[12]

The language, images, and conceptual frames—discourse—that describe and convey a phenomenon like sex trafficking not only circulate between sites such as government documents, media coverage, academic studies, and nonprofit, nongovernmental literatures, but also establish discursive parameters—that is, the frameworks and narratives that demarcate and define a phenomena even as it is being described. The fact that global sex trafficking is a phenomenon described by former United States district attorney of Minnesota Rachel Paulose as difficult to quantify, define, and track[13]—difficult to know because of its hidden and widespread nature—begs the question of the significance of the production and circulation of knowledge. That is, if as Michel Foucault illuminates, knowledge and discourse are sites of power where what is purportedly described in discursive sites (for instance, sexually deviant behaviors) is actually produced through the very discourses that claim to discover and diagnose, then examining the ways discourses define, describe, and address its subjects can reveal important aspects of the workings of power in the shaping of realities.

Language is important not only in shifting mind-sets and perspectives, as Miller notes, but also as a component in the broader discourse circulating about human rights and gender violence that sets conditions as to which activities can be recognized as women's human rights violations and who is then legible as the subjects of those activities. Discourse works to set what Laura Kang terms the "compositional conditions" that shape how we understand an issue like global sex trafficking. Rather than "unveiling some truth that has been misrepresented," this book considers sex trafficking in order to "foreground the particular historical circumstances, ideological suppositions, and methodological tactics that enable and constrain [the] compositional instance."[14] Miller's call to be more attentive to the way we describe trafficking is a major part of this book. However, while Miller draws attention to the fact that language shapes how we see and understand trafficking victims (whether we feel they are simply sex workers or whether we recognize them as slaves), what this book addresses are the ways mainstream institutions like the government, news media, nongovernmental organizations—some of the major institutional stakeholders and players that help shape antitrafficking policies—participate in setting the terms through which the public comes to know and understand trafficking as a human rights violation. These terms hide and naturalize assumptions and understandings of gender, sexuality, race, and nation. Particular scripts and narratives get attached to sex trafficking, and these can reveal the ideas and assumptions that gain political and cultural salience in the debate around citizenship and human rights.

Trafficking is about immigration as much as it is about human rights and gender violence. Looking at the images, language, and frameworks through which a national discourse of sex trafficking is produced can make clear the ways gender norms and racial stereotypes naturalize particular figures of the national subject and citizen. As Eithne Luibhéid, Martha Gardner, and others illustrate, the history of immigration lawmaking and enforcement is one where particular expectations of gendered behaviors and expressions of sexuality were at once produced and policed as central to defining desirable citizenry. These gendered expectations and expressions of sexuality further helped define the racial parameters of the national body, where race was understood as inheritable and therefore always about sex—about miscegenation and marriage, and about sexuality and gender norms. While the VTVPA is seemingly primarily about human rights, it is also equally about immigration and the policing and shaping of citizenry, both in terms of the potential victims who are given the opportunity to become legal residents and citizens and in terms of the construction of the U.S. citizen who helps combat trafficking through gendered and racialized terms. This might explain why there is particular fervor, especially when it comes to state actors, over trafficking for sexual labor, because issues of immigration and citizenship have historically always been accompanied by anxieties over the notion that the "wrong" bodies are reproducing national subjects (an anxiety manifest in 2010 debates over repealing the Fourteenth Amendment out of fears of "anchor babies," for example).

The danger of ignoring the productive power of discourse is evident in the double bind placed on victims who are usually identified as third world, mostly women. These women must argue their own victimization to an economically corrupt, morally backward culture of patriarchy in order to be legible to government officials, law enforcement, and social service providers as trafficked subjects. Becoming legible is necessary to garnering aid like legal status, food, and shelter. Not only does the discourse of sex trafficking risk reproducing the troubling dichotomy of third world backwardness and United States progressivism, as Inderpal Grewal notes,[15] but victims must also often reiterate this construction in their attempts to become legible to government officials and law enforcement as deserving of aid. What are the terms through which subjects can become legible as victims of trafficking? What do these terms tell us about the ways gender, sexuality, and race are working to help shape notions of national and global belonging?

Feminist Stakes, Human Rights, and Modern Conditions

The complicity of human rights projects and many feminisms (sometimes labeled liberal or Western) in furthering and reproducing troubling, uneven relationships of power is symptomatic of a continued investment in modern notions of humanity and emancipation established through Enlightenment and post-Enlightenment texts—epistemological conditions through which contemporary notions of *human* and *woman* are produced that have yet to be adequately deconstructed by human rights scholars. Thus, even while this book is critical of the ways feminisms can and do remain complicit with nation-building projects, it is with a feminist lens that the book approaches women's human rights, trafficking, and the limits of emancipation.

Like the concept of *human,* the category *woman* is vexed by the fact that it is by definition a broad term used to refer to quite a number of people who may have very different relationships to the category. The use of such broad and ambiguous terms like *woman* has not been without political and social advantages, as large numbers of people have been able to stage political claims calling for more attentiveness to patriarchy, for instance, by uniting under the banner of women. After all, there is power in numbers, especially when it comes to agitating for institutional or structural change. Yet the trouble with categories like *human* and *woman* is that despite (or because of) their ambiguity, they nonetheless need to gesture to a particular way of being—a way of being that is always already prescribed at the conceptual moment of modern knowledge. At once referring to universality, concepts like *woman* convey a sameness and sharedness even while the category is itself defined through a particularity and difference from what it is not (man). This is the central paradox of human rights and global feminisms: such terms necessarily convey a particular set of definitions (sometimes multiple definitions) even while they imply nonparticularity and universality.

This paradoxical operation is what lies at the center of human rights debates: how and what gets defined as a human right is not in fact always as universal as the term might imply. What for one community is a human right may not be for another. This has been particularly vexing for feminists who find that nationalisms depend on the prioritizing of heteropatriarchy, yet are unable to critique the global scope of patriarchal investments without risking accusations of universalizing so-called Western notions of gender and human rights. Thus, coming to a global consensus around what rights count as human rights continues to be a contentious exercise and one that is implicated in a long global history of uneven relationships of power, where the project of defining human rights acts as yet another site where colonial relations of power find renewed life. As scholars like Sally Engle Merry point out, the legacy of the European Enlightenment cannot be separated from the concept of *rights* and *human rights*. Some human rights scholars like John Charvet and Elisa Kaczynska-Nay work from the premise that this liberal tradition at the center of human rights is something to be embraced rather than questioned.[16] This book takes the position that such liberal traditions, which arise from epistemological frameworks established in Enlightenment and post-Enlightenment texts, are exactly the reason why human rights threaten to reestablish so-called old hierarchies. How can we address the fact that gender violence does indeed seem to have a global resonance without rehearsing troubling dichotomies of Western progressivism and third world backwardness? How useful is human rights as a site through which to address global gender violence, given the fact that human rights talk threatens to resurrect these colonial configurations of power? Moving beyond the question of human rights as both potentially positive in altering material conditions and negative in reaffirming (neo)colonial hierarchies requires consideration of the conceptual paradox and epistemological terms that frame the notion of human rights.

The questions that circulate in debates around the efficacy of human rights—questions having to do with who establishes what counts in a universal set of principles—resonate with more domestic debates in the United States regarding post–civil rights politics advocating inclusion of difference and the eradication of racism. One of the strongest critiques of human rights has come from actors identified with the so-called third world who are critical of the ways the human rights agenda often reasserts Western privilege and priorities. One strategy used to respond to these concerns involves including those "other" voices into the dialogue, in a sense translating across difference to find common ground. A similar strategy characterizes the successes of the civil rights era, which were organized primarily around responding to the prior strategy of assimilating and/or eradicating difference by advocating inclusion and (equal) representation.[17]

The struggle for the civil and political rights of historically disenfranchised populations has been staged in terms of inclusion and representation on the basis of the acknowledgment that these populations can speak for themselves about what they need and want. Yet while electing women into political office is a necessary and invaluable project, the fact that representation enables the marked body (which signifies difference) to stand in for the correcting of racism and patriarchy is deeply troubling. Under this paradigm for understanding difference and power, the visibility of the marked physical body provides, to borrow Rachel Lee's words, a racial alibi signaling the progressive end to all those things (racism, patriarchy, xenophobia, religious fundamentalism) that are seen as roadblocks to emancipation.[18] Emancipation is defined here as the ultimate nonexclusionary position. The "surely we are not racist, for we accept a black man as president" logic has thus too often been used as a panacea for the still-vibrant landscape of American racism that defines U.S. social relations. As Chandra Mohanty and Jacqui Alexander expertly note, it is deeply troubling when the physical body (as a signifier of difference) is assumed to stand in for the correcting of a body of knowledge: "Token inclusion of our texts without reconceptualizing the whole white, middle-class, gendered knowledge base effectively absorbs and silences us."[19] For Radhika Coomaraswamy and other feminists interested in making the terms of women's human rights a decolonizing (rather than colonizing) tool, remedying the tokenizing of third world women's voices can take place through better dialogue: "What we need today is internal dialogue, first among women in third world societies and then between the women and the larger community. Outsiders must promote and aid this dialogue, giving their support so that such a dialogue is open, rich, and transformative."[20] Yet there is the risk of tokenism whenever an outside and inside community is assumed. This book takes tokenism as a symptom of the modern ontological conditions through which humanity and difference are written and explores the extent to which inclusion through dialogue offers a productive human rights tool.

Conflating physical bodies (demarcated as different) with bodies of knowledge that address difference is one of the overarching concerns of this book. This conflation enables the (visible) inclusion of certain speaking bodies to act as an alibi that allows us to reassure ourselves that we are moving forward—moving beyond. Yet this function of inclusion, which enables the myth of universality, does not disrupt or question the underlying conditions of subjectivity established in Enlightenment and post-Enlightenment texts. Women's human rights is implicated in this progressive, modern narrative as the so-called final global site where the resolution of all those roadblocks impeding emancipation must be addressed, and it is the "othered" bodies of the women victim to human rights violations that are signified as the last and latest subjects awaiting freedom, writing the third world, female body "as the final frontier—as [representing] our temporal and global end."[21] This representational effect is explored through an examination of sex trafficking as one discursive site where Enlightenment legacies and their contradictions shape how trafficking is defined and who is legible as trafficked subject.

Chapters

Human rights is confronted with the fact that, rather than offering refuge to the disenfranchised global subject, it can act as another scene of violence. Chapter 1 considers the conceptual terms through which human rights is framed in order to tease out the epistemological and ontological premises that prescribe human rights mechanisms like the VTVPA. The Universal Declaration of Human Rights, drafted in the post–World War II moment, is often cited as the cornerstone and origin of contemporary human rights. Rather than situate temporal origins, this chapter considers the epistemological origins of the contemporary concept of human rights in order to situate strategies like translation that are touted as a means to discover truly universal principles. Thus chapter 1 considers the debates around translation and cultural relativism that continue to shape human rights debates and focuses on the role of the law in naturalizing certain assumptions about human rights. These debates indicate how the idea of human rights is framed primarily through the notion of representation—of representing humanity and representing fairly different cultural definitions of universal principles. The political desire to frame human rights through the question of representation is not surprising; nor is it without its benefits.

However, the framing of human rights through the question of accurate and fair representation limits its potential by postponing efforts to address the paradox of universalism. Chapter 1 considers the paradox of universalism, strategies of translation, and the politics of representation in order to situate the remaining chapters, which map the cultural and legal scripts that get attached to trafficking.

Chapters 2, 3, 4, and 5 look specifically at the case of sex trafficking in order to map the ways that the making of sex trafficking into a legal and cultural reality establishes assumptions about humanity, morality, and difference that are then taken for granted and constrain the ways we can imagine human rights. Together, these chapters consider the naturalizing of certain gendered, sexual, and racial scripts and the impact of taking such scripts for granted. Chapter 2 situates U.S. antitrafficking law within the historical context of both sexual violence and immigration laws. The law and the legal space is one place where particular scripts of victimization are produced and validated, becoming the institutional standard through which potential trafficking subjects (mainly victims and perpetrators) are judged. Institutionalizing methods used to validate victims, including the requirement that victims testify in instances where their traffickers are prosecuted, means that victims must make their stories fit into preexisting expectations and narratives in order to be legible as victims (rather than prostitutes or illegal aliens). This chapter thus also considers the ways the strategy of speaking for oneself and claiming voice have obscured the relationship between speech and the speaking subject, allowing us to assume a false transparency between the speaking subject and her words.

The victim narratives the U.S. government assumes are the most common and natural narratives that should accompany the violence of sex trafficking are not only produced through studies funded by federal grant dollars and government publications, but also circulate in the literature of nongovernmental organizations and the news media. The circulation of these victim narratives between sites is sometimes a direct relationship where funds made available through the VTVPA finance the research of nonprofits and nongovernmental organizations. Even when these relationships are indirect, no site is insulated from the others. Chapter 3 looks at the ways journalistic accounts naturalize a particular narrative of victimization, one that is surprisingly similar and not surprisingly resonates with other familiar narrative tropes like the

American Dream. This chapter works to understand how telling the story of sex trafficking does more than identify or disidentify potential victims; it frames trafficking through moral tropes of rescue and redemption that ultimately work to naturalize an understanding of cultural difference that reaffirms troubling frameworks of development and progress.

Chapter 4 considers how these developmental frames help make and depend on gender and sexual discourses that naturalize the idea that behavioral and cultural proclivities can be read on the physical body. By focusing specifically on various visual images used to promote antitrafficking efforts (including campaigns sponsored by the Department of Health and Human Services, Immigration and Customs Enforcement, and the United Nations Office of Drugs and Crime) as well as state and NGO research into explaining geographical and cultural origins to sex trafficking, this chapter considers the ways antitrafficking efforts in the United States both echo and help shape understandings of race, nation, gender, and sexuality. Specifically, this chapter considers the juxtaposition of the Eastern European to the Asian victim in order to consider the racial conditions of inclusion through which sex trafficking narratives are articulated.

Looking at the productive power of sex trafficking discourse illuminates the racial, gendered, and national stakes tied to making distinctions between human bodies—between the victims in need of human rights and the human rights enacting subject. For the most part, discussions of human rights have to do with how to define universal principles and how to enact and enforce such principles. There is much generative debate around the issue of whether it is possible to outline principles that can be applied universally. While many postcolonial and feminist human rights advocates are critical of the ways androcentric, Euro-American, or Western values are taken for granted as universal, the question of race remains relatively marginal as difference is articulated through the language and frame of culture and nation. The literature on race and race relations is one that often centers the national, and global studies of race tend to compare one national formation to another. By drawing out the connection between what is often considered a domestic issue tied to identity politics in the United States (race relations) and the question of universalism and cultural relativism that is central to discussions of human rights, chapter 5 considers how talk around human rights in the United States is necessarily informed by the national context. Conversely, the language and framework of difference, inclusion, and pluralism central to domestic discourses of race have found their way into international forums like the United Nations. Domestic discourses around difference and race, while seemingly distanced from debates around human rights, are in fact two conversations that enable each other. That is, contemporary national discourses of racial difference, particularly multiculturalism and postracialism, are made available through the concept of human rights and global diversity. Alternately, contemporary human rights discourses share much of the language, frameworks, and strategies for understanding difference that U.S. civil rights–era activisms articulated. Chapter 5 looks specifically at the ways sex trafficking references the language and history of transatlantic slavery and argues that such uses work to consolidate multicultural and postracial narratives of racial and gender progress in both the national and global context. Sex trafficking thus works to consolidate a national narrative of exceptionalism that universalizes the U.S. condition.

The conclusion considers these questions of knowledge, power, and human rights through a transnational feminist lens. Transnational feminism can offer a useful methodological tool to mapping how power works to shape social norms and realities by pressing for the need to deconstruct and understand the relationship between nation making and the production of discourses of difference. By understanding race, gender, sexuality, and nation as conceptual tools that work co-constitutively (the concepts and categories help define each other), feminist methodologies can do more than simply describe experiences; they can help map the ways regimes of knowledge—concepts, frameworks, and discourses—help make social realities.

By looking at how sex trafficking is talked about and what assumptions are naturalized in talking about it in a particular manner, this book suggests many alternative ways of seeing that go unheeded. The chapters in this book are interested in interrogating the gendered and racialized nation-making work women's human rights agendas like sex trafficking perform in order to fully consider whether (given the ways the sex trafficking discourses circulating in the United States rehearse neocolonial power dynamics and rely on liberal notions of rights) women's human rights can offer a generative and useful site through which to address the global complexion of gender violence. In doing so, the discursive analysis suggests various alternative ways of reading sex trafficking texts. This is not to suggest that there is any one correct way of understanding sex trafficking as a human rights violation or the impact it can have on the people who experience and live it. Rather, the book poses a variety of alternative readings in order to demonstrate what can get lost or ignored when we are not attentive to the assumptions and premises at work in naturalizing narratives as "the sex trafficking narrative."

Undoubtedly human rights have offered a productive mechanism through which to confront modern maladies, and certainly there are people all over the globe who find use in human rights as a tool for addressing injustice. Yet human rights as a modern discourse is not immune from the very modern maladies it hopes to confront. This is why understanding the onto-epistemological roots of human rights is crucial, and it is by looking to sex trafficking that the racial, sexual, and national stakes tied to particular ways of knowing and being can be made clear. Excavating the intellectual traditions and modern premises established in the philosophical debates around natural law, humanity, and rights is a necessary exercise in considering how the concept of human rights can be recuperated as a useful political tool, given the fact that human rights is always overdetermined by this modern genealogy. Looking at how certain activities are produced and defined as sex trafficking reveals the implicit ways our discussions of human rights fall back on assumptions about subjects, their "others," and definitions of freedom and rights that reaffirm the ideas of humanity set forth in seventeenth- and eighteenth-century European philosophical texts on man. Understanding these philosophical limits is crucial to the task of rethinking human rights.

1. Universalism and the Conceptual Limits to Human Rights

IN THE POST–WORLD WAR II cold war context of 1948, the recently formed United Nations adopted a Universal Declaration of Human Rights (UDHR) to help instill a global sense of community founded in the principle of humanism. Yet even before its formal adoption, the idea of any UDHR was confronted with questions of how to know a universal tenet of human rights from a particular cultural expression. While this post–World War II–era context provides the formal origin of contemporary human rights language and frameworks, the concept of universal principles evoked in the UDHR echoes the philosophical and political projects of empire building that defined the nineteenth century, rooted in modern regimes of knowledge. The question of universalism at the heart of contemporary human rights debates is informed by this legacy of empire and colonialism, which naturalized the so-called progressiveness of certain political, economic, and epistemic principles under the banner of the universal.

Despite the displacement of formal colonial governments and the rise of independence movements during the early twentieth-century human rights era, the systems of knowledge that enabled colonialism, transatlantic slavery, and Euro-American empire building remain intact. This is evident in the way human rights agendas continue to fall into the trap of reproducing troubling representations of "others." This operation of human rights has been critiqued as taking place in various human rights sites, from the plight of the Roma in Europe,[1] to the representation of African women in debates concerning female genital surgeries,[2] to the veiling of Muslim women.[3] The representational impact of colonial logics and frameworks continues to plague international discourses from development to human rights. This chapter attempts to answer why human rights continues to offer a site where (neo)colonial relationships of power are rehearsed and suggests that the reasons are embedded in the conceptualizing of universalism against

1

a notion of cultural relativism, where (cultural) difference becomes both the condition of universalism's possibility and a threat to its existence. Universalism is defined here as a distinctly modern concept that regulates descriptions of both social and scientific life.

This problematic of difference lies at the crux of human rights debates around how to define universal principles and how to represent the varied victims of abuses. Both the question of how to ensure respect for (cultural) difference and how to keep from reifying constructions of third world backwardness have been answered in part by inclusionary strategies like translation and cross-cultural dialogue that advocate representation of all so-named culturally particular views and previously marginalized players. However, the crux of the problem of difference comes before the question of accurate and equal representation; it lies rather at the moment of the conferring of subjectivity and humanity, a moment that (ontologically) precedes representation, though the representational moment helps constitute the conditions attached to the conferring of subjectivity.

Inclusion reproduces, though not without contradictions, the conditions of subjectivity instituted in modern, post-Enlightenment regimes of knowledge. These conditions of subjectivity establish an enabling negation—an "other" against which the modern man is constituted. Modern regimes of power are also instituted through the juridical realm and continue to inform contemporary understandings of humanity, subjectivity, and the law. Representation and inclusion are thus strategies limited in their ability to intervene in the workings of power that produce (neo)colonial regimes because these strategies assume universality; that is, these strategies assume that with greater representation and more inclusion, we will be able to more accurately locate universal principles of humanity. Rather, universalism itself needs to be denaturalized and understood as a modern concept that helps structure how we know and understand human rights.

Human rights seem unable to leave behind the onto-epistemological conditions that result in the re-presentation of colonial logics casting third world peoples and practices as less advanced and therefore less capable of enacting human rights principles. This chapter addresses the conceptual and theoretical workings of the writing of human rights and its subject. By situating feminist debates grappling with the question of whether and to what extent the notion of women's rights can serve as the basis for a shared international agenda, the chapter establishes the paradox of universalism. Last, the chapter situates this paradox within an epistemological context that confers universality through the juridical frame, which then works to naturalize colonial logics. Understanding and examining how we come to know what we know is, in other words, central to addressing the paradox of human rights that leaves human rights rehearsing and reifying, rather than addressing and correcting uneven relationships of power.

The Conditions of Universality

The UDHR established and enumerated the rights all persons are entitled to by virtue of being human. Drafted by eighteen members of the United Nations Commission on Human Rights, chaired by Eleanor Roosevelt, and written in response to the atrocities of World War II, the declaration is described by the United Nations as a "living document" that has "stood the test of time and resisted attacks based on 'relativism.'"[4] One year before the 1948 adoption of the UDHR, the board of the American Anthropological Association released the following statement regarding the challenge of relativity associated with drafting the UDHR:

Respect for differences between cultures is validated by the scientific fact that no technique of qualitatively evaluating cultures has been discovered. . . . Standards and values are relative to the culture from which they derive so that any attempt to formulate postulates that grow out of beliefs or moral codes of one culture must to that extent detract from the applicability of any Declaration of Human Rights to mankind as a whole.[5]

Coming out of the relativist turn, the statement of the Anthropological Association affirms the work of Franz Boaz that attempted to shift evolutionary notions of human difference (as racial science and the science of man) away from seeing difference as innate and biological to seeing difference as cultural. Advocating an understanding of difference that foregrounded culture as a matter of consciousness, the relativist turn, established through Boaz's work and crystallized in the Anthropological Association's statement, maintains universalism but locates it in the universal existence of culture and cultural systems. In essence, universalism is defined as both the many cultural systems differentiating peoples and as more than the sum of these cultural systems. Mindful of the importance of cultural relativism, the authors and supporters of the UDHR thus emphasize that the document's articles are not reflective of the "beliefs or moral codes of one culture" but are instead universal; it is a document that "belongs to all of us" in similar ways that all of us belong to culture.[6]

The historical significance of these two documents reveals how talk around human rights emerges with and through discussions regarding cultural relativism. As the drafters of the UDHR worked to conceptualize a statement of rights that was broad and yet also applicable to a variety of national, legal, and cultural contexts, they also contributed to an important conversation around Eurocentrism and representational ethics. For the Anthropological Association, the risks of any Declaration of Human Rights rest in the possibility that under the guise of the universal, the declaration would implicitly evaluate cultures against the cultural norms represented in the declaration. In other words, the concerns of the Anthropological Association were about whether a universal declaration would be able to maintain relativism. This context defines human rights and universalism as concepts constituted through difference and particularity. That is, the idea of universalism for both cultural relativists and advocates of a universal declaration is defined by the equitable representation of (cultural) differences, leaving universalism in the paradoxical position of inventing and maintaining (culturally particular) "others" while also needing to absorb them.

Thus one way that the drafters of the UDHR attempted to address the need for cultural relativism was to include and represent a variety of rights that would together make up a set of universal principles. The articulation of these principles begins with a first generation of rights modeled after (and both theoretically and linguistically similar to) the tradition set forth in the English Bill of Rights (1689).[7] These statements read in familiar ways to the United States Constitution, naming rights to which individuals are entitled by virtue of being reasoned and self-conscious:

Article 1. All human beings are born free and equal in dignity and rights. They are endowed with reason and conscience and should act towards one another in a spirit of brotherhood. . . . Article 2. Everyone is entitled to all the rights and freedoms set forth in this Declaration, without distinction of any kind, such as race, colour, sex, language, religion, political or other opinion,

national or social origin, property, birth or other status. . . . Article 3. Everyone has the right to life, liberty and security of person.[8]

Built on the Enlightenment tradition of rational law, these rights are
framed in terms of protections from state interference and encroachment on individual freedoms. Other articles include the right to equality before the Law (Article 7), the right to be considered innocent until
proven guilty (Article 11), and the right to own property (Article 17).

Given that these first twenty or so articles are derivative of a liberal,
Euro-American tradition, the framers of the UDHR included a second
set of rights derived from socialist revolutions as well as a third set of
articles that are more aspirational in nature.[9] These second and third
groupings of rights are framed in positive terms and require state intervention. Rather than envision a rights-bearing individual in need of
protection from state encroachment, these rights—the right to social
security (Article 22), the right to rest and leisure (Article 25), the right
to education (Article 26), and so on—are framed in terms of state re-
sponsibilities toward its citizenry. Furthermore, the third set of rights
moves away from even the framework of the state by naming community as the organizational unit—for instance, the right to participate
in the cultural life of community (Article 27) and community duties
essential to free and full development (Article 29). This move away
from the Enlightenment language and traditions of liberal individualism and the social contract is evidence of the compromises the framers
made to ensure that they avoided "formulat[ing] postulates that grow
out of beliefs or moral codes of one culture," as the Anthropological
Association warned.

Yet even as it seeks to represent in a relativist manner several different approaches and ideologies to principles of humanity, the UDHR
also seeks to absorb these different approaches into a universal standard that privileges the dominant perspectives of the modern liberal
traditions of the social contract (dominant even in terms of the number of articles that privilege this frame). Advocating the UDHR as "a
common standard of achievement for all peoples and all nations," the
ultimate goal of the document is to enumerate and uphold a universal standard against which "all peoples and all nations" should strive.
Whether the UDHR succeeds in capturing a set of rights that do not
grow out of the "beliefs or moral codes of one culture" was and continues

to be a hotly contested question, especially given that Article 1 defines human beings as "endowed with reason and conscience . . . born free and equal in dignity and rights, precisely the definition established through Enlightenment texts."

Furthermore, enforcing a global rule of law to ensure the principles of the declaration is not an easy task. Assuming that controversy over how the document defines human rights is resolved, such measures to address violations still face the fact that there is no extrastate institution that can enforce the document. Indeed, one key limitation of the United Nations lies in its inability to do more than place political pressure on states that choose not to comply. Thus, almost by default, the UDHR and other human rights vehicles ultimately rely on individual state mechanisms for operationalization. In the case of trafficking, despite the U.N. Protocol on Human Trafficking and the frameworks, lenses, and concepts it deploys to define activities as trafficking, states provide the units through which the protocol is mechanized. In the United States, this mechanism is the VTVPA. The degree to which the spirit of the protocol is maintained (and whether it is even adopted into state legislation at all) remains under the purview of the state, though NGOs play an important role in convincing "powerful audiences . . . that the right deserves acceptance."[10] It is the state's claim to the force of law that gives the state the legitimacy it needs to both deploy violence and restrict freedoms necessary in the policing, prosecution, and punishment of activities like trafficking in protecting human rights.

The law offers both a tool and legitimizing force to the state, and it can only do so because the concept of the law is one mythologized around the fact that the law "transcends society yet is of society."[11] Like the concept of universalism, the law is mired in a contradiction where it is both an institution made by men even as it also surpasses human creation. Men make the law, yet the law exists as a thing beyond man's creation. Such a formulation is a hallmark of the modern epistemologies established through Enlightenment and post-Enlightenment texts. As Bruno Latour catalogs, the dual constitution of politics (the social) against nature (science) is accompanied by a second operation whereby science hides the fact that it is a construct of man and politics hides the fact that it is treated as a force of nature.[12] This formulation, according to Latour, defines the modern. To understand the (modern) predicament of human rights, subsequent sections of this chapter consider the ways politics and the law are defined as social products even as they function as forces of nature. This continued working of law and politics, following Latour, places contemporary human rights and trafficking squarely within modern frames. Philosophers like John Locke rationalized a distinction between the transcendent force of law that makes it above all men and the rational application of that force that is the product of society. Rendering human development a teleology that casts man in a linear story from a savage state of nature to the moment of the social contract and onward into the unfolding of civilization, the tradition Locke helped instill establishes a project of modernity, one where the subject is constituted over and against his nonmodern "others." The law emerges as a force that is known through reason and accepted by the reasonable subject as transcendent—transcending any particular social or political context. Global "others" who did not grasp this fact were simply cast as behind. Thus at the heart of human rights are questions pertaining to the universality of the law. The concept of universality, defined as more than the sum of its particular components—a something that captures everything, institutes the particular even as it is also threatened by it. Defined in opposition to the particular, universality cannot exist without the concept of the particular where "no assertion of universality takes place apart from a cultural norm."[13] The universal operates as a modern strategy of power that continues to write the "others" of the globe as "not yet," thereby naturalizing the modern regimes of knowledge that privilege the self-knowing and rational subject. The project of human rights becomes one where those not yet exercising the freedoms associated with human rights simply need to reform cultural values, economic relations, and legal institutions—reformatory outcomes of the actualization of the kind of being (subjectivity) produced in the post-Enlightenment text.

Representational Limits: The Paradox of Women's Human Rights

The early 1990s saw the rise of the concept of women's human rights in the international political arena, most notably with the 1995 United Nations Beijing Conference on Women. The 1995 conference is remembered as a milestone event that marked the ascendance of women's human rights on both national and international agendas, and as an event that evidenced the growing global call for the celebration of human diversity. Yet the project to define women's human rights has a long history predating the 1995 conference—a history marked not only by the United Nations' Decade of Women, but myriad nongovernmental and grassroots organizing. These political and social projects that focus on addressing gender violence on a global scale inform and are informed by intellectual debates around feminism and the study of women. That is, academic and intellectual projects like the disciplining of Women and Gender Studies that are interested in understanding the category *woman* and the concepts of gender and sexuality have been both an important outgrowth of political organizing and social movements as well as an important venue where political concerns gain ground.

The idea that there should be better attention to women's human rights in part arose out of feminist critiques of human rights discourses that, these critiques argued, worked from androcentric assumptions about the subject of rights. Arguing that existing human rights paradigms are formulated from an unacknowledged gender and sexual bias, feminist critics argued the need to amend these frameworks to better capture gender-specific human rights violations like "rape (including marital rape and rape during war), domestic violence, reproductive freedom, the valuation of childcare and other domestic labor as work, and unequal opportunity for women and girls in education, employment, housing, credit, and health care."[14] Feminist human rights scholars like Susan Okin, Hillary Charlesworth, and Charlotte Bunch identify a possible solution to issues of androcentrism as the inclusion of women's voices and experiences. As Charlesworth notes, "We must work to ensure that women's voices find a public audience, to reorient the boundaries of mainstream human rights law so that it incorporates an understanding of the world from the perspective of the socially subjugated."[15] Coinciding with the critiques of human right's Western (cultural) bias, these feminist critiques argue that centering women's experiences can highlight the ways androcentric and Eurocentric assumptions inform the definitions of human from which the idea of human rights works.

The focus on experience, while incredibly generative, has nonetheless left open the question of whether there is any generic woman's experience. As calls to center women's experiences within human rights violations and gendered violence brought forth a wide variety of experiences, debate around the universalizing of the category (woman) brought to the forefront an old dilemma: To what extent can the category *woman* work as a universalizing tool through which to gain political strength? The idea of a common category can work to emphasize the need for a shared agenda across national, cultural, racial, and economic differences. At the same time, the use of *woman* as a tool through which to make common claims also emphasizes differences, where such a move might simply rehearse a "politics of virtue" where help is not "freely given; there must be . . . some evidence that those receiving help are in fact deserving of help," a move that exposes the uneven relationships among women that enable some women to speak for all women.[16] Women's human rights thus simultaneously connotes the promise of solidarity across difference and the reimposition of colonial relationships, where "'American' feminists [are situated] as saviors and rescuers of 'oppressed women' elsewhere within a 'global' economy run by a few powerful states."[17]

Patriarchy may be global in its scope, yet it is not universal in form. This has made defining women's human rights difficult, as the project straddles the fact that what women's human rights might mean for women may differ from context to context even while the driving impetus is one that recognizes that women can share similar experiences under patriarchy. Thus third world feminists have continued to take issue with global feminisms that uncritically assume all women should desire similar goals (usually tied to freedom and other monolithic concepts defined through Euro-American, often liberal, philosophical traditions). Even so, third world feminists also stress the importance of recognizing the potential power of organizing around the global aspects of gender-based violence. As Vasuki Nesiah notes, the human rights framework "has been an enabling framework, internationalizing rights discourse and thereby opening space to engage with the struggles of 'Third World' women. On the other hand, it has been restrictive. The struggles of 'Third World' women have been conceptualized only within the narrow vocabulary and institutional framework of rights discourse."[18] Not recognizing the ways patriarchies are racialized and differentially constructed, or the ways feminisms can work to free some women at the cost of others enables human rights to further reassert neocolonial relationships.

Human rights and feminisms grapple with this paradox—categories of difference like *woman* cannot help but impose sameness across the category, even while there is a desire to recognize the particularities of experiences within the category. On the one hand, such categories are not arbitrary. They have been historically deployed in such ways as to create sameness and shared experiences (evident, for example, in the experience of the transatlantic slave trade that racialized people from all across Africa as black). On the other hand, fighting against the workings of power that homogenize difference (into a uniform, categorical understanding of women, for example) has often taken the form of emphasizing the heterogeneity within such categories of difference, of demonstrating precisely the arbitrary nature of the imposition of these categories. Put a different way, the concept of universality is constituted through that of particularity, even as the concepts are defined in opposition to each other. Hence conceptualizing claims to universality necessarily require the concept of particularity (against which universal claims are defined) even as claims to universality must disavow the particular. The result of this paradoxical operation is evident in claims to global diversity that desire to recognize and protect difference and particularity, even as they advocate that these particularities are subordinate to a broader order of universality.

Gender violence has a global resonance, yet calls for women's human rights or even claims made against patriarchy cannot account for the multiplicity of ways rights, patriarchy, and even woman as a category are understood and inhabited. However, abandoning calls for recognition (of women, of women's rights) across national and cultural differences diminishes the wide-reaching impact of gender violence. Shefali Desai perhaps poses the dilemma of feminisms and human rights best when she notes:

In evaluating an Afghan woman's refugee and asylum claim, feminist theory can embrace neither cultural relativism and send the claimant back to her country thus implying that the Taliban's laws regulating women's lives are merely an expression of culture, nor universalism that would grant the claimant refugee status but fail to question the universality of internationally established women's human rights standards. The former addresses critiques of feminism as merely another form of imperialism, but leaves feminism without a standard by which to "condemn abuses of women throughout the world." . . . Meanwhile, the latter solution declares that all women suffer from patriarchal oppression and that the way out of this oppression is by applying an established set of human rights to the asylum claim. It offers "the promise of uniting women," but risks the oppressive essentialism that feminist theory seeks to combat.[19]

Articulating a tension that lies at the heart of feminist theorizing, organizing, and activism, Desai ponders the conundrum of universalism and relativism that operates on multiple scales—from the academic feminist debate around identity, experience, and difference to the concerns of human rights organizations working to forge connections across and between borders without privileging Western cultural lenses and priorities.

Desai's interest in refugee and asylum claims also points to the significance of human rights as a potential site where feminist interventions and concerns might positively foster actions that reduce the day-to-day impact of gendered violence. At the same time, it opens and encourages theorizing of the extent to which "woman as human" is a useful claim and the extent to which any claim or call that assumes a universal standard can address questions of violence. The conundrum for feminist theorizing that Desai articulates grapples with the necessity of addressing both a material violence—for Desai, one that is signified through the example of "the Taliban's laws regulating women's lives"— and a representational and epistemic one that threatens to rehearse the troubling operations of power that characterize and enable imperialism, colonialism, orientalism, essentialism, and so on.

Neither a claim to universal principles nor a claim to cultural relativism adequately addresses the global aspect of gendered violence. Echoing concerns articulated by feminists like Uma Narayan about the inadequacy of both "the imposition of Sameness"—that is, universalizing claims that sisterhood is global—and an "insistence on Difference" that characterized the colonial encounter,[20] Desai cautions against any uncritical acceptance of feminism as divorced from imperial and colonial projects. However, recognizing the ways feminism can act as another site of imperial/colonial power "leaves feminism without a standard by which to 'condemn abuses of women throughout the world.'" One suggestion Desai offers to manage this dilemma is to listen and hear "Afghan women's voices . . . while concurrently contextualizing the experiences being heard," where Afghan women's voices are heard even as they are contextualized as "occupy[ing] relatively privileged positions because they were in a situation where they could be heard."[21] While the importance of including and recognizing voices previously excluded cannot be understated, hearing and including "other" voices cannot alone serve as an end-all strategy for social justice. One of the reasons why inclusion is an incomplete strategy is captured in Desai's recognition that "although more and more voices are becoming a part of women's human rights discourse, there are voices that have not yet been heard and some that may never be heard."[22]

For one, representational strategies pose difficulties in terms of mechanization because there is no end to the multitudinous voices waiting to be heard, as Desai acknowledges. These strategies of representational inclusion also defer interrogations into the paradox of universality that ultimately limit human rights projects. By maintaining the distinction between speaker and listener, the strategy of hearing voices risks being reduced to claims of authenticity. If the multitude of voices can never be heard, then there is a need to establish authentic voices that might be representative of a given experience. Under such assumptions, dissenting voices can easily be labeled less authentic and therefore relegated to less importance. For example, what happens when Afghan women speak both for and against Taliban practices? What happens when it is one voice that simultaneously supports and rejects the Taliban? Such positions often become untenable or dismissed as uninformed, disingenuous, or inauthentic. Thinking of these voices as simply misguided or censored is too simplistic an answer to the dilemma Desai poses. One side may argue that certain laws imposed by the Taliban regime inflict gender violence, while another side may argue that such a view comes from an ignorant position that does not appreciate different cultural norms. Both claims are true, and both sides can produce "native speakers" who attest to the validity of each side. Where, then, are human rights and feminist critiques left?

Negotiating the dilemma of human rights—the dilemma of universalism—through the institutional recognition of the individual voice, where one woman's definition of gender violence can differ from another without taking away from the idea of the global aspect of patriarchy privileges liberal principles of individualism. While it is admirably diplomatic to suggest that conflicting claims around gender violence can be equally true (the Taliban inflict gendered violence, the Taliban protect women), such privileging of individual experiences and claims can stifle arguments about the broader-reaching mechanisms of power that work by homogenizing and impacting communities rather than individuals. When Afghan women critique U.S. military intervention justified by the project of spreading women's rights or when Afghan women support the Taliban, how can we understand these positions without reducing them to matters of individual perspective that foreclose arguments about the global inflection of gendered violence and neocolonial relationships? Answering such a question requires deconstructing the conceptual principles that are more often than not taken for granted in human rights talk, conceptual principles that privilege modern, post-Enlightenment understandings of humanity, difference, and the law.

Translating Human Rights: Negotiating Relativism

While feminist discourses have called for attentiveness to difference, this very call has then been turned around and used to reinforce the status quo, to justify patriarchal practices beneath claims to cultural relativism. For example, in the case of the Taliban, the call for diversity and attentiveness to cultural relativity has been used to justify practices that inflict gendered violence. At what point is the claim to cultural relativism simply a rhetorical device used to maintain harmful practices? At what point are claims to cultural relativism valid in their critique of biases hidden within calls for universal principles and human rights? These questions regarding the role of relativity and particularity to human rights are often answered through the advocating of translation as a means to respect cultural particularism while also generating a set of universal principles.

A strategy related to inclusion translation, as a means of uncovering shared principles across different (cultural) contexts, is limited because it addresses a moment that comes too late. The fact that "translation by itself can also work in full complicity with the logic of colonial expansion when translation becomes the instrument through which dominant values are transposed into the language of the subordinated,"[23] is an effect of the conceptual terms established in the taking for granted of universalism. In other words, that translation "can also work in full complicity with the logic of colonial expansion" is a symptom of the modern conditions of knowledge and subjectivity through which the very notion of universality is constituted.

What remains to be considered is the fact that the strategy of translation is already circumscribed by the very conditions of power producing "others" as signifiers of difference (as global particulars). Translation already assumes a kind of transparency, between the speaking subject and the act of speech—an assumption that misses the fact that speech, and strategies of representation in general, is always already mediated by the discursive conditions through which subjectivity is conferred, exemplified most vividly in the desire to elicit the testimonies of trafficking victims. In other words, the language of the subordinated is always already shaped with and through dominant values; there is no pure language of the subordinated. Rather, the language of the subordinated needs to be understood as situated within a discursive landscape shaped through the dynamic and dialectical relationship between what gets labeled as subordinate and dominant.

Translation is thus an instrument that enables universality, and universality is that which underwrites modern regimes of power. Thus strategies of translation and questions of translatability come too late in the sense that they assume the very conditions of power they hope to challenge. In the example of debates surrounding Islamic law, translation becomes a way to protect the idea of Islamic law (as a cultural particular) while still condemning its specific application. This is one way to negotiate the need to uphold cultural particularities like Islam, which shape societies as different, while still condemning this very particularity for being different and thereby insisting on universalism. For example, in a 2001 congressional hearing held just after the attack on September 11, House representative Ileana Ros-Lehtinen (R-Fla.) articulates the issue of Islam and cultural relativism this way:

In 1996, a heavy shroud was placed on the people of Afghanistan when the Taliban captured Kabul. Since then, the Taliban has taken the peaceful and sacred scriptures of the Prophet Muhammad, and distorted them into a rulebook of terror. . . . The Taliban is far from being students of the true Muslim faith. . . . The U.S. role is not to dictate what a post-Taliban government will look like. Our role is to empower and enable, in order to ensure that the true and unfettered voice of the Afghan people is heard loudly and clearly.[24]

Ros-Lethinen's framing keeps from vilifying Islam as a whole by suggesting that the Taliban regime distorts the "peaceful and sacred scriptures." Here the cultural particularities of Islam and Islamic law are perverted in the Taliban's specific translation and interpretation of the Qur'an. Playing on the idea of authenticity, Ros-Lethinen's framing negotiates particularity by implying that the true voices of the Afghan people remain unrepresented and unheard as a result of the Taliban. By suggesting that regimes like the Taliban simply translate the Qur'an in patriarchal and repressive ways, translation arguments can defer the paradox of universality by simultaneously condemning particularity while also upholding it.

The desire to maintain universality and a conception of universal human rights, and the conflict it faces in the midst of claims to relativism, thus informs the move to (re)cast the issue of particularity as a matter of dialogue and translation. In another example, Abdullahi Ahmed An-Na'im notes that maintaining an international system of order situated within a (diverse) landscape of localities means that

the norms of the international system should be validated in terms of the values and institution of each culture, and also in terms of shared or similar values and institutions of all cultures. This can be achieved, I suggest, through what I call "internal discourse" within the framework of each culture, and "cross-cultural dialogue" among the various cultural traditions of the world.[25]

Like many others, the solution that An-Na'im proposes is one premised on the belief that proper "internal" and "cross-cultural" dialogue "among the various cultural traditions of the world" will yield a more accurate sense of universal principles. For An-Na'im, each culture must engage in "internal discourse" discussing what values should be validated. The inclusion of "other" voices is key here in bringing to the forefront (of their own cultures and governments, as well those of the rest of the world) those values or cultural traditions that should or should not be deemed universal. Thus critiques of cultural practices begin within the cultural community.

This is a powerful strategy in the ways it attempts to recenter debates around human rights and universalism on those communities that in the past had been marginalized in such decisions and discussions. However, it is also a strategy that works only with the assumption that so-called cultural communities are discrete and bounded entities, an assumption the limits of which are well documented by anthropologists and legal scholars critical of the use of culture as a (legal) defense.[26] This position does not have a way to address the fact that concepts, frameworks, and value systems are not bound to (cultural, geographic) communities. In fact, so-called cultural actors (whether so-called in-siders or outsiders) define a cultural community or tradition as such through a dynamic process that works through both what is perceived to be "our" cultural tradition and what is perceived as "theirs."

While an understandable desire, these calls to discover or establish universal principles by attempting to more accurately represent the various "contesting norms that constitute the international field," work from the already presupposed and taken for granted notion of univer-sality. Rather than interrogate the production of the very concept of the universal, calls to locate universality can never adequately consider the regimes of knowledge that have instituted the universal within both the realm of transparency and the juridical frame. The solution of dialogue operates to ensure the mythic quality of universality; uni-versal principles and values guiding human rights are constructed as coming out of the social process of dialogue, even while that dialogue must already be in line with a preexisting notion of universal princi-ples. The revelation of this mythic component is subsumed into its very narrative unfolding; the notion of dialogue ensures that the threat of relativism to universal rights is rendered a moment in the issuing of uni-versality. The dilemma here is that the values validated through cross-cultural dialogue are exactly those values that enable cross-cultural dialogue. Universal principles are assumed to be transcendent; they are simply reaffirmed as universal by being reflected back through inter-nal dialogue. While this moment of mirroring and reiteration can be read as holding the potential of "contamination and displacement"[27] of the original term or terms being translated, the conditions of con-tamination and displacement are already constricted. Thus, altering existing paradigms, frameworks, and mechanisms is always a rather slow, contested process of negotiation.

Modern Foundations: Human Rights and the Limits of Law

The desire to locate universal principles through translation—dialogue between different groups—presupposes the conditions of difference that are assumed to impede human rights projects. The presupposition of particularity/difference takes for granted the operations of power that write universality as a real and discoverable object rather than as a conceptual mechanism and myth that structures how human rights can be framed and understood. This is why debates around how to define human rights continue to replay the same conversations. How do we represent difference and different cultural values while still upholding universal principles? How can we avoid establishing universal principles that normalize or take for granted a dominant (often Western) perspective? How do we avoid reestablishing colonial relationships in the quest to ensure human rights? Questions such as these, important and valid as they are, are outcomes of the taking for granted of the principle of universality as a transcendent aspiration in opposition to the (sometimes clouded) operations of particular cultural values.

The modern regime of power established in the Enlightenment and post-Enlightenment projects that sought to explain the nature of man and his difference from things, animals, and slaves posited the notion of humanity as universally defined by his capacity to reason, his ability to exist as self-conscious, and his recognition of the rule of law. These three aspects determined the conferring of subjectivity between men as well as distinguished men from nonhuman things. As the philosophers of man reasoned about those attributes distinguishing man, they were most concerned with describing the conditions around them: the condition of Europe.[28] The most complex society, handled by the most rational of men and demonstrating the rule of law, was located in exactly that place where these philosophers of man were situated: Western Europe. The writing of this subject as the model of humanity envisioned this subject as universal—a standard against which all other consciousnesses and subjectivities could be measured. Thus one key hallmark of the modern episteme, of the paradigms of knowledge established in Enlightenment and post-Enlightenment texts on man, is an understanding of man (the human) as he who knows his difference from what he is not (his "others"), a formulation memorably accounted in Hegel's reconciliation of the subject with his constitutive outside.[29]

Reason, in these accounts, enables self-knowing by governing (and producing) the interior mind of man, where man is situated as a self-knowing subject in his recognition of himself over the course of time (temporal scene) and against what he is not (spatial scene).[30] Thus subjectivity is constituted, in Hegel's work, for instance, through the interiority of the rational mind, which can distinguish himself from his past and future self, and through the exteriority of the distinction he can make between himself and the (nonhuman) things of nature. As

Denise Ferriera da Silva catalogs, these premises established modern subjectivity through a moment of consolidation when man realizes that the things outside him signal a moment in the actualization of his self-consciousness and mind. It was Hegel's rationalization of those other things of nature that enabled modern (European) men to reconcile the existence of the nonrational others of Europe (natives, slaves, colonial others) as "enabling others" that only existed to affirm the humanity of the self-knowing subject. Hence non-Europeans were established as the less rational "others" of Europe, who exist within this figuring only to enable the actualization of modern, enlightened rationality: "A central promise of Enlightenment and Western modernity is that conflicts between knowledge and power can be overcome by grounding claims to and the exercise of authority in reason. . . . [Reason] operates identically in each subject and it can grasp laws that are objectively true."[31] This writing of the post-Enlightenment European subject as a universal standard of mankind is enabled through the conceptualizing of the rule of law as both a product of men's actions (social) even as it exists above and beyond the scope of the society of men (transcendent). So long as the law and reason are transcendent and all, even global "others," are subject to them, the particular project of European modernity could write its own legal systems as global models.

The universalizing of the project of European modernity can also be apprehended by understanding the ways the law negotiated the contradictions of the social contract and freedom. For Locke and others, the absolute state of freedom or nature is always imagined to be in constant negotiation with the desire for peace—a peace that cannot be instituted without governance (which draws its legitimacy from Law).[32] Natural rights are thus always sacrificed to some extent to ensure civil society, whether this sacrifice happens out of fear of anarchy or out of desire for peace. This understanding of society establishes the law as crucial to negotiating civil society, to negotiating freedom for peace (or mutual freedom). The law's mythological aspect as universal and beyond man's creation ensures the idea of freedom; man is subject to the law, but because the law is not man's creation, he remains free. At the same time, man's laws are necessary to maintain peace, for instance to keep men from killing each other, which cannot happen without sacrificing freedom. Thus the law restricts freedom to ensure freedom. Historically, this contradiction of freedom at the heart of social contract theories has justified slavery and colonialism, where the freedoms of some (the enslaved, the colonized, the native) were viewed as necessarily repressed or forfeited for the benefit of peace. In other words, slavery is not necessarily antithetical to freedom, given the contradiction of freedom instituted through modern knowledge. Thus the story of the social contract hinges on the simultaneous writing in and writing out of an "other" that represents a state of man before the reasoned apprehension of laws.

The majority of work on human rights generated out of disciplines like political science and international relations defines human rights in terms of the struggle and negotiation of the state (civil society) with natural law/rights (human rights). In this context, human rights are defined as universal, moral, ethical, natural rights—rights that extend beyond the state or the contracts of the civil society. Charlotte Bunch describes human rights "as inalienable," rights that "no one can voluntarily abdicate . . . since those are rights which we have by virtue of being human."[33] In this sense, human rights as natural rights are beyond the legitimate governance of the state where the state can only ensure their protection, but cannot restrict their exercise. Human rights thus produce a global context beyond the boundaries of the state and always already assume the human as subject to (state) juridical governance.

The law thus works as the precondition to global civil society, and it is the function of the law as simultaneously man's creation and not man's creation that institutes human rights as a modern project. In order to reconcile the "contradiction between [law's] autonomy and law's social dependence," the law must be elevated to the realm of myth and given a mythological quality in its "transcendence of its own myth of origin where it is imperiously set against certain 'others' who concentrate the qualities it opposes."[34] The move to rationalize law as both a socially interpreted set of rules as well as a universal force necessitates a figure (an "other") that stands before the law, both in the temporal and epistemological sense. The possibility that this premodern enabling other might eventually learn to properly apprehend human rights and join global civil society reconciles the law as both particular (social) and universal (transcendent).[35] It is the possibility of the "other's" inclusion into the (correct) legal systems—into civilization and human rights—that makes possible the contradictory aspects of the law. Thus the conditions that enable the "other" are not dismantled in the inclusionary moment; rather, the inclusionary moment is simply another chapter in a modern regime of knowledge. Problematic relations of power and privilege remain because the strategy of inclusion cannot dismantle, because it is a part of the actualization of, the very operations of modern subject formation that constitute difference/particularity in the first place. Even while the law is definitive to the modern narrative and enables the power and authority of modern knowledge, it is also able to hide this constitutive relation. It is the universal and transcendent definition of the law that operates to define human rights as a moral matter beyond reproach, while the social/practical definition and deployment of the law is seen as that which must be changed (in certain cultural circumstances). So long as definitions of human rights assume a framework that dichotomizes it as a matter of moral law posited against culturally particular interpretations and legal systems that may or may not protect human rights, it remains limited in its ability to address justice.

In the context of human rights, the law is often assumed a universal tool (that is, a tool that all humans recognize) that can, when perverted, violate human rights, or, when deployed, properly protect them. This fundamental assumption about the transparency of the law is one that also restricts understanding the limits of the law itself. So long as human rights assumes the frame of the social contract and natural law (law as surpassing human creation), which is posited against rational law (law as human creation), it remains decidedly trapped to rehearse and re-enact (neo)colonial relationships. So long as human rights assumes a framing that defines universalism as both the sum of and more than the sum of its particular (cultural) components, it remains mired in the modern condition, left to ask the same questions again and again: "Is this universal? Can we discover universal principles through translating across particular cultural contexts?" What needs to be better addressed in discussions of human right is the way human rights assumes and institutes modern regimes of knowledge and subjectivity. This chapter attempts to make a compelling argument for why such work is necessary.

Attending to Absences

These conceptual foundations are evident in the ways they structure representations of human rights abuses like sex trafficking. To demonstrate the ways assumptions around human rights enacting subjectivities are reflected in the framing of antitrafficking representations and are shaped by such representations, the chapter concludes by considering an antitrafficking United Nations Office of Drugs and Crime–produced public service announcement (PSA), "Open Your Eyes to Human Trafficking" (2008).[36] The most recent of a series of antitrafficking announcements ("Cleaning Woman," 1998, 2003; "Work Abroad," 2001; "Better Future," 2002; "Telephone," 2003), "Open Your Eyes" was released as part of the Global Initiative to Fight Human Trafficking, and it demonstrates the ways the taking for granted of modern and liberal principles restricts the ways human rights can be represented.

"Open Your Eyes" begins with an image of an older white man walking down the streets of an outdoor marketplace. The specific locale of the marketplace is ambiguous, though it is represented as a multicultural space where white, black, and brown bodies provide the background. The white male protagonist is shown shopping at the various market stalls. His first encounter is one where he sees an overweight white man, standing and eating french fries and a sandwich in a greedy manner, as food falls onto the sidewalk. This man is presented as unkempt, from the food stains on his clothes to his unshaven face. Behind him are two men, one white and one black, both skeletal in frame, lifting and moving boxes. The camera pans suggest that the two men working in the background work for the overweight man in the foreground. As the scene shifts, the two skeletal men are depicted eating the dropped food left on the sidewalk by the now absent overweight man.

In the next encounter, the announcement depicts the protagonist smiling at a young black boy, who is sitting on the sidewalk panhandling. The protagonist then nods to acknowledge another older white man whom he passes as he walks down the street. After nodding back to the protagonist, this other white man forcefully grabs the arm of the sitting black child as he scoops the money into his plate and takes the boy away. In the protagonist's final encounter, he watches from a distance another older white man in a business suit talking to a woman in the doorway of a small business. Inside the building is a younger woman sitting on a chair, looking forlorn. Both women are nonwhite, perhaps Central South Asian. As the protagonist looks on, the other white man exchanges bills with the woman and walks into the room with the girl, closing the door behind him. While the earlier scenes present the protagonist smiling and enjoying himself, in the final scene, he glances over his shoulder with a concerned look, suggesting that he has finally opened his eyes. The announcement ends in a white screen with text reading "open your eyes to human trafficking," leaving the viewer to wonder what, if anything, the protagonist might do. The announcement contains no dialogue, and the only text that accompanies it reads, "It's a hidden crime. It's happening all around us," ending in the final sentence, "Open your eyes to human trafficking." The music accompanying the announcement is the refrain to "Wonderful Life," a 1987 song by British pop band Black, which sings, "No need to run or hide; it's a wonderful, wonderful life. No need to laugh or cry; it's a wonderful, wonderful life."

Creating a clear distinction between the (human rights) actor holding the potential for change and the passive victims waiting for help, viewers are assumed to identify and sympathize with the white older man who is the announcement's protagonist. That the protagonist is marked (through race, mobility, dress) as similar to the traffickers and victimizers allows the announcement to draw a moral distinction between the at-first-unaware protagonist and his criminal counterparts. The victims depicted in the announcement represent the widely circulated assumptions around the different kinds of victims trafficked for different forms of labor: men trafficking for bonded labor, children trafficked for various types of exploitation, and women trafficked for sexual labor. It is the final moment, when the announcement's protagonist witnesses the girl trafficked for sex, that he begins to question what he has been looking at but not seeing. The announcement, which never suggests what leads the victims into their condition as trafficked subject, works to prioritize the moral lens in representing and understanding trafficking, which asks the privileged presumed first world traveler to "open his eyes."

While there is only one female victim represented in this announcement, read together with the other PSAs, particularly "Cleaning Woman" and "Telephone," the significance of the racial and national frames distinguishing female victims of sex trafficking implied in the announcements points to the conditions attached to how human rights subjectivities can be framed. "Cleaning Woman" is an announcement similar to "Open Your Eyes" in that it is directed toward white, presumed first world subjects (whether they might potentially help rescue victims or exploit them).[37] It appeals to a sense of moral obligations among women to help save (racially, nationally) other women who are victimized through sex trafficking. "Telephone" is the only PSA directed toward the trafficked subject and depicts three characters, one African, one Asian, and one Latin American woman, who are sex-trafficking victims breaking free and calling a United Nations help line. "Cleaning Woman" and "Telephone," as PSAs specifically addressing sex trafficking, were aired on American Forces Network, a television station dedicated to U.S. armed-service personnel stationed abroad in places like South Korea. This message is in line with U.S. Department of Defense documents that chronicle the efforts undertaken to implement a zero tolerance policy on trafficking, which includes "training . . . for every military person that goes overseas, educating him on this [trafficking for sexual labor] issue."[38] Amid criticism that militarism abroad participates in, rather than combats, trafficking activities by fueling demand for sexual services, the U.S. Department of Defense has undertaken this high-profile zero-tolerance campaign issued in 2002 by President Bush.[39] As part of these measures, the effort in South Korea is coupled with the U.N. public service announcements.

While there is much to laud about the DOD's recent efforts to combat the soliciting of sexual services by service personnel stationed abroad, these efforts in large part focus on reforming individuals, a message also represented in the U.N. announcements that focus on white male and female rescuers or nonwhite individual victimized women. Rather than question the structural mechanisms behind militarism that operate on and help perpetuate heteronormative regulatory ideals around masculinity and the necessity of (state) violence,[40] DOD responses to military prostitution and intimate and sexual violence focus instead on reforming the moral obligations of individual soldiers (that is, good men protect women's sexuality). Further, as Meghana Nayak points out in her examination of DOD efforts since the late 1980s to address sexual violence (for instance, relationship violence, harassment, and rape), these efforts actually "limit sociopolitical recognition [of sexual violence] in several ways. First, sexual violence only matters to the extent that it interferes with the military's progress in being 'mission-ready.' . . . Second, the actual experiences of all survivors of military violence are not represented [in the existing military mechanisms to address such violence]. . . . Third, the responses fail to thoroughly and diligently understand why sexual violence occurs."[41]

In the U.N. anti-sex-trafficking announcements, the female victims are represented through their sexualized vulnerability as sex slaves marked also through their racial difference as not white. Because there is no gesture to suggest the conditions that lead to trafficking (only the moral frame distinguishing criminals from victims and potential rescuers), the announcements keep viewers from questioning the role of structural factors like militarism and global circulations of capital in enabling trafficking. The victims in "Telephone," "Cleaning Woman," and "Open Your Eyes" are all suggested to be victims in part because they are not allowed to work as formalized members of the economy and therefore have no formal means to ensure protection from labor abuses (they are undocumented laborers, panhandlers, and sex workers). Coupled with the representation of criminals and exploiters as individuals (the overweight man, the other white man, the woman running the brothel, and the man in the business suit), "Open Your Eyes" fails to implicate corporate capital and businesses as also enabling trafficking activities. Furthermore, this framing does little to trouble the fact that undocumented labor (labor with no legal protections), whether coerced or not, has been a necessary feature that has historically enabled capital accumulation and profit. Put another way, if "Open Your Eyes" suggested more strongly that the protagonist's participation in the multicultural marketplace is not so distanced from that of his antagonist counterparts who traffic, exploit, and solicit, the representation of trafficking might shift to implicate a different set of questions: How do global mechanisms of capitalism enable and shape trafficking activities? How do they naturalize certain forms of labor over others? How does capital accumulation depend on undocumented and unregulated labor of all kinds? What makes some work legitimate but not others? Is migration ever a choice?

Thinking about trafficking through lenses that focus on interrogating existing (legal, human rights) paradigms for understanding migration threatens to question the structural ways current political, legal, and economic modes of relations institutionalize the need for less formal and therefore less regulated kinds of work. Rather, the focus of "Open Your Eyes" around the difference between the unaware traveler and consumer who might potentially be a rescuer and his various knowing yet morally corrupt counterparts makes trafficking a matter of suspect cultures and individual moral capacities. The register of race that is sometimes used to distinguish the protagonist from the trafficked victims (and in the case of sex trafficking, the brothel owner negotiating with the white male john) works to gesture to the absent yet implied presence of the cultures from which the victims were trafficked. While the criminal traffickers and johns are represented in the announcement, "Open Your Eyes" suggests the there are other criminals left unrepresented: people or contexts that enabled the victims to be trafficked in the first place, whether they are family members or cultural conditions that leave victims little choice.

These "culpable cultures" are significant in that they reveal the conditions of inclusion and the conditions of universality[42]—conditions that require a difference against which subjectivity can be conferred. The victims in the announcements must be saved in order to ensure the inclusionary impulse of modernity's universality. Yet the conditions of subjectivity offered through the announcement require an enabling negation, an "other" against which the human rights–enacting subject can be defined. If the trafficking victims do not represent this enabling negation, their cultural counterparts back home do. The visual logic linking these victims to the cultural community from which the trafficking narrative originates ties the victims to the very cultures (of patriarchy, of poverty) that lead to victimization, thus establishing the need for outside rescue. By rendering trafficking a matter of moral law and human rights, the inclusion of the global "others" negotiates the fundamental dilemma of liberal theories of rights and law—the tension between universality and particularity. The "other" figures enable the recuperation of the myth of universality by marking the inclusion of particularity even while her victimization to a (deviant) culture (of patriarchy, of poverty, of corrupt values) signals a particularity that must be disavowed. The question is not whether and how the universal can be truly universal in the sense that it reflects more accurately the multitude of differences. The strategy of finding voices or of acknowledging the multitudinous nature of speech in an effort to uncover or even redefine universals that are shared across difference fails to interrogate and deconstruct the distinction between listener and speaker, and between universal and particular, which is the fundamental epistemological issue constraining human rights projects.

One significant drawback to connecting the limits of human rights and the law to epistemological foundations is that this approach can seem hopeless. It is not realistic to simply ignore the conditions of knowledge that shape how to know; ignoring these conditions leaves us with the same dilemmas, of human rights claims being used to reify neocolonial relationships, of the law working to naturalize developmental narratives of progress and backwardness, and of feminisms working against deconstructing power relations. Yet if there is no outside to knowledge—in other words, if these regimes of knowledge always already establish the parameters through which subjects act—then changing such conditions seems an impossible task. The remaining chapters of this book acknowledge these difficulties; however difficult and seemingly hopeless, altering the epistemological conditions through which we know the "real" is not an impossible task. It is a task that requires acknowledging the ways in which what is often categorically dismissed as theoretical, abstract, and ungrounded is in fact a necessary component to the so-called grounded realities of daily life. Thus how we come to know trafficking as such, and what assumptions and frameworks shape conventional understandings of trafficking, are questions the remainder of this book considers.

2. Speaking Subjects, Classifying Consent
Narrating Sexual Violence and Morality through Law

DURING A CONGRESSIONAL hearing on human trafficking held in 2007, Zipora Mazengo, an immigrant from Tanzania who was awarded a T visa, testified to her experiences as a victim of trafficking. She stated that her employers (diplomats) held her for four years, withholding pay and her passport and not allowing her to venture outside their home. Mazengo describes her experience this way:

Once when I did not prepare her [employer] breakfast she hit me on the face and sent me in my summer clothes to stand outside in the snow. She told me that if I complained, "blood would fall on the floor." . . . When my toe became infected [my employers] did not take me to a doctor. My feet bled until I could not wear shoes, but [my employer] made me go outside to shovel snow in bare feet. . . . I agreed to come today to speak to you because I do not want what happened to me to happen to anybody else.[1]

Narratives like Mazengo's proliferate in trafficking documents, though direct testimonies are rarer than representative stories loosely based on true events with fictional victims. Such narratives help illustrate the various contexts of trafficking and help outline victim profiles even when they are fictionalized accounts. For the U.S. Department of State and prosecutors, having victim stories helps to identify and make a case against traffickers. While the kinds of scripts that gain currency in courtrooms and public media are important in validating experiences like Mazengo's, it is also important to examine how some scripts and stories become privileged over others. In part because trafficking is defined as an ambiguous and hidden activity, creating stories that are representative of trafficking abuses is a necessary part of seeing and identifying victims. Yet there is more going on in the production, circulation, and validation of trafficking stories than simply exposing a hidden truth; the ways in which certain scripts gain currency can impose a different form of violence on trafficked subjects, one that is symbolic or representational. For example, in the 2005 *United States v.*

Trakhtenberg case, prosecutors brought charges against alleged traffickers on the basis of evidence that included statements to the police provided by a witness and victim referred to as Eva Petrova. During prosecution proceedings, Petrova refused to testify in court, asserting that her initial statements to the police, which describe her experience as one of victimization, were obtained under threat of deportation.

Contesting the limited terms of representation, Petrova elected to return to Russia before the trial and responded with the following letter to the court (authenticated by a Russian lawyer):

The authorities' reps had forced me to develop a hostile stand with defendants in order to portrait [*sic*] myself as a victim. . . . Many events were presented incorrectly and were grossly exaggerated. . . . They [U.S. law enforcement] told me that if I am not going to cooperate with them, I am going to be charged with alleged illegal entry into the U.S. . . . and that I will be placed in the immigration jail for a long period of time and then deported.[2]

According to Petrova, she and four other women from Russia were smuggled into the United States with the intention of performing sex work in New Jersey and New York. Petrova writes that she does not see herself as a sexually trafficked victim, though she was identified as such by law enforcement.

While there are a plethora of reasons as to why Petrova would feel the need to qualify her statements to the police and law enforcement, what is interesting about her letter is the fact that even though it is evidence that she refuses to see and narrate herself as a victim, her refusal and retraction are nonetheless used by the courts to justify her rescue. Law enforcement initially refused to accept a statement from Petrova that did not portray her as a victim, according to her complaint, and the court ultimately rewarded her $4,280 in restitution as a victim of sex trafficking despite her decision to flee the United States to avoid providing further testimony.[3] The way in which Petrova's concerns were simply cast aside in the final ruling suggests that her objections to her alleged coerced testimony were perceived as simply an insincere attempt to retract as a result of trauma or fear of retribution from her alleged traffickers. Whether this was in fact the case is never an issue the court or law enforcement took up with Petrova. In an ironic turn of events, Petrova stated in a different letter to the court: "I was forced to provide inaccurate and imprecise information about the defendants and certain events. . . . The U.S. authorities' reps instructed me on how to construct conversations in order to obtain statements that authorities needed."[4] Furthermore, Petrova stated that incessant threats made by U.S. authorities to narrate a particular kind of victim narrative caused her to have a nervous breakdown, which certainly calls into question exactly to what circumstances Petrova is victim.

Petrova's case demonstrates the need to situate and analyze existing notions of violence and rights and to reexamine the legal mechanisms in place to "rescue" trafficking subjects. Trafficking prosecution cases like *Trakhtenberg* help shape "individual and collective images of victims and victimization" that work as part of the discursive landscape through which the courts, law enforcement, advocates, and trafficked subjects navigate.[5] Such collective images shape legal and cultural stories that not only help identify sex trafficking, but also define the rhetorical parameters through which trafficked subjects like Petrova can become legible where "meanings [are] created in the courtroom for a larger public."[6] This chapter considers the ways the Victims of Trafficking and Violence Protection Act (VTVPA) has worked to establish a profile of the trafficked victim in order to consider the ways antitrafficking activities might actually impose their own form of violence even as these activities also provide aid and relief. Petrova's case thus illuminates the need to consider not only how victim status is defined and conferred, but whether including potential trafficked subjects into the realm of legally recognized, rights-bearing subjects (as the U.S. state currently imagines it) can be taken as a singular and universal goal toward justice and redress.

This chapter considers how trafficking victims come to be defined and represented through legal and state mechanisms by situating the VTVPA within a historical context of sexual violence and immigration laws. Given that the VTVPA passed as a bill that combined the Trafficking Victims Protection Act (TVPA) with an updated version of the Violence Against Women Act (VAWA originally passed in 1994), sex trafficking is considered within the broader legal frame of sexual violence and can be read as a different kind of rape story, one that implicates illicit border crossings while hiding state violence in policing national borders. How the category of trafficked victim comes to be defined and represented is part of a broader historical process of policing and producing the boundaries of citizenship—processes that are informed by and help shape racial meanings and gender/sexual norms. The chapter considers the impact of linking justice to a trajectory of subjecthood that moves from silenced victim to speaking subject. Given that the courtroom and the stories told there both reflect and help shape cultural understandings of citizenship, this chapter begins to map how a particular victim narrative is shaped through legal and cultural sites, an effort undertaken in subsequent chapters as well.

Trafficking and Sexual Violence

Trafficking, particularly as it is defined in its primary definition as forced or coerced sexual labor, works within existing legal frameworks for understanding the role of consent in intimate and sexual violence crimes. The long U.S. legal history of regulating sex and morality (through marriage, rape, inheritance, obscenity, pornography, prostitution, child care, and other related laws) has worked to establish and ensure patriarchal, economic, and racial privileges.[7] Sex trafficking, insofar as it conjures the image of a victim "chained to a bed in a brothel,"[8] invokes gender, sexual and racialized discourses of morality, criminality, and vulnerability that have also shaped sexual and intimate violence laws, particularly rape laws. While the case-by-case litigation strategies and outcomes vary widely in the many types of crimes labeled sexual and intimate violence, providing the broad strokes of how sexual violence gets framed through the law can establish a useful context to understanding legal and state measures undertaken to separate sex trafficking from other forms of sexual violence. In particular, how the legal components of force and (lack of) consent (and to a lesser extent mens rea or criminal intent) help frame rape as a criminal matter can provide context and demonstrate the contrasting gendered, sexual, national, and racial assumptions that work to inform sex trafficking subjectivity.

Feminist and antirape activists and advocates have drawn attention to the discrepancy in social and legal measures to address rape given its prevalence, and they link rape and its relative disregard by the law to the institutionalizing of sexual violence and power.[9] The legal and criminal definition of rape defines it as sexual intercourse by force and without consent.[10] Traditionally, the courts have privileged physical force as an indicator of lack of consent, and silent compliance has amounted to consent if there was no proof of threat of bodily harm.[11] Legal reforms during the late 1970s ensued in part as a result of feminist and antirape movement activisms. These reforms sought to make rape more visible, particularly "private rape" taking place among non-strangers. These changes to the law were implemented in an effort to make prosecuting intimate violence and rape crimes easier.[12] Specifically, changes to rape law at the state level (in all states) relaxed the ways consent and resistance were defined to allow for reasonable resistance (so a victim does not need to actively fight off an assailant), which tempered traditional approaches that equated resistance to the use of force. While the extent to which individual states define or even require proof of resistance varies, overall changes are aimed at allowing greater flexibility in considering what constitutes resistance and force. Other reforms included repealing corroboration requirements, shield legislation that limits the instances when sexual character could be introduced as evidence, opening up the possibility of marital rape, and eliminating prompt complaint requirements.[13]

As Catharine MacKinnon, Carole Pateman, Meghana Nayak, and others make clear, the public/private frame that operates as a cornerstone of Western legal traditions shapes what forms of violence can be legally recognizable.[14] Historically, this has worked to establish certain relations as private and therefore outside or tangential to so-called public matters of law and politics. Many of the crimes that currently fall under the umbrella of sexual violence have been (and continue to be) difficult to litigate despite legal reforms due to the continued prevalence of the private/public frame as well as the presumption of the reasonable person taken for granted in jurisprudence, evident, for instance, in the historic inability of wives to make any claims of sexual violence against husbands as a result of legal and cultural attitudes that such matters were private. Thus, "in the context of intimate violence, the impulse behind feminist legal arguments [is] to redefine the relationship between the personal and the political, to definitively link violence and gender," particularly when it comes to domestic violence and marital rape where notions of marital privacy have posed challenges to addressing the role of family structures in enabling violence.[15] However, the notion of marital privacy has been unevenly applied, and this is especially true when considering historical instances when so-called private matters between wives and husbands became public concerns, notably when such matters threatened existing racial, class, and gender relations.[16]

One feminist theory of rape that gained salience during the 1970s and 1980s rape-reform activisms thus attempted to define rape as a crime about power and dominance, making rape a public matter. For instance, Susan Brownmiller's work asserts that "although rape involves sex . . . it is not a sex crime but a crime of power and aggression. . . . Through rape or threat of rape, men control women."[17] What was often left unaddressed in these approaches were the ways racial power works to differentiate the context of rape, for example, in cases where the threat of rape has historically allowed white women to control non-white men. Thus despite efforts to reform rape and sexual violence laws so that they better recognize and address gendered violence, the persistence of racialized scripts of feminine vulnerability to masculine aggression are left largely unaddressed due to the court's insistence on a so-called color-blind and neutral approach to the law, which makes the court unwilling to address the ways an "entrenched racism frames the criminal-justice system."[18] One result of this is a "significant gap in the enforcement of crimes committed against [black versus white rape victims]," which is tied both to the underreporting of rape by black women, "prosecutors[' decisions to] decline to pursue black women's rape allegations for a variety of reasons, ranging from their own prejudice to the prejudice of juries that may render such cases unwinnable," and the overenforcement of the law in the criminalizing of black perpetrators.[19] Thus the persistence of particular kinds of rape stories— "a plausible story that not only fits with the [presented] facts, but also resonates with the juror's life experience"[20]—in the courtroom helps shape and validate, and also reflects, racialized understandings of gender/sexual norms, making some rape cases more publically compelling than others.

The salience of certain kinds of rape stories both in the cultural and legal realms—interracial rape, rape of white women, stranger rape, rape accompanied by beating—plays on and helps perpetuate racialized understandings of sexuality. For instance, following the work of Angela Davis, Valerie Smith's examination of the cultural narratives of high-profile interracial rapes situates cases like the 1989 Central Park jogger within the discursive frames established through slave owner property right legacies, lynching and antilynching arguments, and the antirape feminist movements of the 1970s to show how the linking of "sexual violence with racial oppression continue[s] to determine the nature of public responses to them."[21] Contrasting this well-publicized case, which involved a young white woman who was allegedly raped and beaten by a group of Puerto Rican and black men while jogging through Central Park, to the treatment of rape cases like Tawana Brawley's, which involve black female rape victims, Smith suggests that the hypervisibility of certain cultural narratives and rape stories are tied to a historical, ideological legacy "that protected white male property rights by constructing black males as rapists, constructed black women as sexually voracious" and white women as sexually vulnerable, where "the rape of a black woman becomes a contradiction in terms."[22] Relatedly, the circulation of rape stories in both nationalist and colonial ventures has worked as a metaphor for colonial relations where "either the Native woman is taken up as a helpless [rape] victim of her own people in need of rescue by the superior white men, or white women, presumably endangered by the presence of racialized men, is the catalyst for intervention by white men. In any case, rescue narratives revolve around the presumed weakness of women, whether Native or European, and the moral superiority of white men."[23]

Legal definitions and mechanisms help shape cultural understandings of intimate violence and rape, where scripts of victimization develop through both the arguments and testimonies validated in the courtroom and through media and cultural sites, which help shape and are shaped by courtroom scripts. The way the courts and legal proceedings help validate certain kinds of racial and gendered scripts is evident in the media focus on both "stranger rape" and rape through physical force. Echoing these more traditional and sensational representations of rape and sexual violence, the VTVPA definition of trafficking specifies that coercion is primarily indicated through physical restraint and abuse or the threat of it.[24] Thus popular representations of sex trafficking work from similar assumptions around force and nonconsent as leaving physical (and emotional) indications on victim's bodies, privileging the image of a woman "chained to a bed in a brothel," which can pose difficulties for trafficked subjects hoping to gain legal recognition but fall outside this picture. As Dina Haynes points out, when law enforcement "officials subscribe overtly or covertly to unhelpful myths about the nature of victims and criminals," they risk treating "trafficked persons as criminals, particularly when the victim does not fit into the expected mold of being rescued after being found chained to a bed in a brothel."[25] Furthermore, the fact that the legal mechanism put in place through the VTVPA requires that victims be certified and found by government officials neglects to consider that "most victims of human trafficking are not 'rescued' by anyone . . . [but] find their own way out of their situation."[26]

Rape laws provide a vexing yet rich site for feminist legal critics interested in exposing the conceptual limits of the U.S. legal mechanism and framework. For one, the basic assumptions taken for granted in rape laws already assume a passive, racialized female subject vulnerable to an active (aggressive) male one.[27] The element of mens rea adds to this aspect by focusing on the mind and intentions of the alleged perpetrator to be measured against the principle of the reasoned person; thus the intentions of the accused are often pitted against the physical state of the victim's body, further reinforcing gendered notions of aggressiveness and passivity. That is, the legal treatment of rape plays to and naturalizes gendered expectations (passive femininity, aggressive masculinity), which makes it difficult to consider rape through contexts that fall outside a heteronormative lens, thus privileging rape stories where women are victim to men. The criminalizing of rape also hinges on an implied innocent victim who is at least more innocent than the alleged perpetrator. This makes it difficult to see, let alone prosecute rape, among criminalized populations—for instance, the rape of prisoners, undocumented persons, sex workers, and the homeless and transient, as well as in cases where alleged perpetrators are associated with law enforcement.

Sex trafficking provides a rape story that implicates undocumented immigration but hides stories of border-patrol rape. Given that sex trafficking narratives focus predominantly on nonnational victims, the hypervisibility of sex trafficking as a rape narrative hides the fact that rape among undocumented persons (and those who fall outside state legal protections in general) is virtually ignored (at least legally) in all other situations. For instance, rape committed by border-patrol personnel can be considered a form of militarized "national security rape" that remains unrepresentable because of the criminalizing of undocumented persons as well as the taken-for-granted legitimacy of state violence.[28] Sex trafficking as a rape narrative implicating undocumented victims is more easily represented, even when it involves traffickers and perpetrators who are associated with law enforcements (for instance, involving United Nations peacekeeers or U.S. military personnel), in part because trafficking has been framed through the prism of human rights over that of national security. Yet sex trafficking and border-patrol rape stories are both about policing and shaping national borders.

Like rape stories, narratives of sex trafficking highlight the need to construct victims as innocent and worthy, and the privileging of the rational person principle—of an individual legal subject defined by her capacity to consent, choose, and eventually testify. Because sex trafficking stories implicate Asian, Latin American, and African (as well as Eastern European) victims, these narratives shift racial scripts around the unrapeable, oversexed nonwhite female that have historically circulated in rape cases and resulted in a cultural discrepancy between representations of rape cases involving white versus nonwhite, especially black victims. Similar to the treatment of rape, sex trafficking works by assuming and producing a subject who is victim precisely because of his or her lack of consent, though in contrast this lack of consent is/ need not be not proven in court as with rape cases, only validated by a Health and Human Services officer through a process that takes place outside the court. In fact, once such validation takes place, as the case of Eva Petrova demonstrates, it is difficult to retract even during court testimony and proceedings. Aware of what it takes to gain recognition as a victim, trafficked subjects often recount narratives that fit into already accepted scripts. Thus testimonies reveal more about the conditions under which they are given than anything else.

Sex Trafficking or Prostitution? Policing National Belonging

Assumptions about the moral and sexual character of the individual play a key role in the process established to certify genuine trafficking victims from illegal immigrants. The U.S. government uses the term *smuggling* to refer to individuals who consent to cross into the country. In such cases, those being smuggled are considered responsible for breaking the law, while in cases of trafficking, victims are not. Because authenticated victims are offered the possibility of applying for legal status, who gets to claim this status is a question wrought with anxieties concerning who can make claim to the nation. Though reauthorizations of the VTVPA emphasize that domestic trafficking takes place in staggering numbers, the kind of moral panic tied to trafficking across national borders is one that has made trafficking of undocumented persons hypervisible.

The anxieties surrounding foreign bodies as potential trafficking subjects has historical resonance with the general fear of the threat of moral and sexual degeneracy of immigrants. For example, as Jo Doezema notes, the specific panic around "white slavery" during the Progressive Era was tied to the fear of "foreign impurities" (notably Chinese American men) to white racial purity.[29] Such sentiments helped pass the Mann Act (also known as the white slavery act) in 1910 but are also discernible in the much longer history of immigration law dating to the Page Act of 1875, which assumed that the physical body produced visible markers of morality (again, notably targeting Chinese immigrants). Similarly, the VTVPA also reproduces links between the body, racial otherness, and sexual deviancy, resulting in the sorting of worthy victims that reinscribes assumptions of sexual character in racialized terms.

Conceptualizations of who can make claim to the nation have since the nation's founding been anchored in claims to morality and fitness, where the perceived sexual morality of women in particular served as the gauge for determining the conditions of entry and citizenship. This is true both in terms of immigration laws and the policing of ports of entry,[30] as well as the state's investment in validating certain kinds of marriages to help uphold both the color-line and gender norms.[31] Before the turn of the twentieth century and the panic around white slavery, the term *sex slave* was used as a derogatory slur directed at the supposed moral depravity of Japanese and Chinese women seeking entry. Fear of racialized sex slaves helped to direct and justify exclusionary immigration policy from the enforcement of the Page Act to the eventual overturning of the Gentleman's Agreement over fear that Japanese prostitutes were gaining entry disguised as wives.[32]

This fear during the turn of the twentieth century—that Asian women would gain entry as fake wives—not only implies that such suspect women are prostitutes, but also finds resonance in some of the contemporary trafficking literature that implicates the mail-order-bride business as possible fronts for sex trafficking. Both the mail-order-bride business and trafficking grapple with similar issues tied to globalization, citizenship, and gender/sexuality,[33] as acknowledged by the U.S. Department of State, which has included a small section on mail-order brides in the 2008 and 2009 *Trafficking in Persons Report*. It is certainly possible that individuals find themselves in trafficked situations under the guise of marriage. It is equally possible that mail-order brides fully consent and agree to marriage arrangements and are not trafficked. What is interesting in the desire to implicate mail-order brides as potential sex trafficking victims is that it illuminates the ways policing of marriage through moral appeals (rather than legal ones) uphold regulatory norms of marriage as love-based relationships. In other words, seeing the mail-order-bride industry as potentially hiding sex trafficking works to affirm assumptions about marriage as primarily entered into out of a notion of love, cultivated through interactions that span a respectable time frame and include face-to-face meetings (which many mail-order marriages do). This is not to undermine the troubling assumptions of patriarchy, commodified sexualities, and global capitalist relations that naturalize uneven distribution of resources on which the mail-order-bride industry operates. Rather, it is simply to demonstrate another way the sentiment of respectable and legitimate marriage as based on love (however unrealistic) works as a regulatory norm to police national borders and the boundaries of citizenship.

The policing of borders through the practice of sorting marriages as legitimate (love based) or illegitimate has a long history, where U.S. immigration officials sorted suspect marriages from "real" ones in a manner that was informed by official's preexisting racial and cultural biases and that helped create discourses of sexual and moral delinquency as a racial matter. For example, in the case of Chinese immigrants during the nineteenth century, even when wives had proper legal paperwork recognizable to U.S. officials that validated their marriages, they were still subject to various techniques, including medical examinations and interviews, through which immigration officials confirmed the validity of marriage certificates. Women hoping to enter as wives essentially needed to prove their respectability.[34]

Derogatory usage of the term *sex slave* to indicate immigration fraud was used initially to refer to Asian women, and it played on the unrapeable aspect of women of color in a moral appeal to block entry of Asian women.[35] However, by the Progressive Era (1890–1920), the landscape of racial formation and immigration shifted significantly to allow sympathy for some "white ethnic" immigrants and some poor and working-class whites.[36] During this time, the term *sex slave* lost its previous derogatory meanings and was used instead to refer to the potential (rape) threat to white women. For the first time, "the use of 'slavery' to characterize the arrival of 'white' women" helped distinguish who could make claim to the category *white,* as well as cemented the "assumption that prostitution could be linked to racialized ethnic categories."[37] The passage of the Mann Act to protect white sex slaves was one of several state documents (including the Dillingham Commission Report) that helped racialize whiteness as sometimes including "white ethnic" immigrants, racialized white femininity as deserving and capable of reform, reaffirmed gender norms that naturalized white women's dependent and vulnerable status, and reasserted heterosexual, monoracial marriage as a regulatory norm.

In similar ways, even while the language of the VTVPA shifts to seem less exclusionary and xenophobic when compared to historical predecessors, trafficking discourse continues to produce national subjectivity through the idea of moral and sexual fitness. The definition of trafficking acknowledges that there are many forms of labor in which victims find themselves, yet sex trafficking takes a front seat in both media attention and the law; sex trafficking is, after all, the first definition of trafficking enumerated in the VTVPA. Trafficking can take place under myriad conditions; however, one particular image of the woman or child trafficked into sexual labor remains hypervisible in mainstream representations of trafficking.[38] Sex not only sells, but it also has a long legal history tied to both moral panic and enforcement of procreative sex. This history of legislation around sex has helped to construct the idea of sex as mutually exclusive of work, where sex work is constructed as abhorrent and thereby criminalized.

Rather than recognize sex work as a form of legitimate labor and exchange, enforcement of the VTVPA takes a prohibitionist stance that links prostitution to trafficking.[39] This prohibitionist stance has been enforced to greater and lesser extent, usually depending on the political leanings of the presidential office. For example, during the Bush administration, an organizations' ability to qualify for both VTVPA funds and USAID was tied to a requirement that these organizations make a public declaration opposing sex work and prostitution. *DKT International v. United States Agency for International Development* is one case where refusal to make a public declaration condemning sex work led to the retraction of USAID funds. DKT, a nongovernmental organization in Vietnam that provides family planning and HIV/AIDS prevention programming, argued that a public prohibitionist declaration would stigmatize clients, many self-identified sex workers, with whom the organization works. Heard in 2007 during the Bush administration, DKT lost its case. The prohibitionist stance of the VTVPA in part explains why the Bush administration and conservative Christian interests have joined with traditionally more liberal political factions in making sex trafficking a bipartisan women's human rights issue of national concern.[40] As a result, transitions between Republican and Democratic administrations and majorities have been relatively smooth in terms of antitrafficking policy.

The VTVPA approach to trafficking emphasizes sex trafficking and wrestles with the impulse to read all sex work as potential trafficking cases and with controlling borders (including moral ones) as part of regulating immigration and citizenry. The tension between the desire to read all prostitution as sex trafficking while also regulating citizenry and immigration results in the at once liberal extension of rights and restrictive requirements for authentication. The authentication process thus implicitly creates and relies on a distinction between worthy victims and unworthy prostitutes even while the VTVPA is anchored in frameworks of prostitution that link it to trafficking.[41] This implicit distinction separating out respectable and worthy victims is one reason for the relatively low numbers of recorded victims actually aided by the law in comparison to estimates of the number of individuals who are trafficked in the United States.[42] Potential victims are evaluated through, and thus help normalize, certain "gendered images of vulnerability" that "[focus] on women and [foreground] their vulnerability along with children's vulnerability."[43]

The VTVPA institutionalizes a certification process to authenticate real from false victims. The process begins with local law enforcement and concerned community members, including social service providers like health-care professionals, counselors, teachers, and vigilant individuals. These individuals bring suspicious activities and potential victims to the attention of district attorneys, who then inform the Department of Health and Human Services (DHHS). DHHS officials investigate trafficking claims alongside local law enforcement and issue certification letters to anyone the DHHS deems is a victim of trafficking. Certification letters enable individuals to apply for aid like temporary shelter and food assistance (the same assistance and terms granted to refugees). Letters also allow individuals to apply for formal immigration status through Homeland Security. Victims generally apply first for continued presence (CP), which extends temporary approval to remain in the United States. They then have the opportunity to apply for a special T visa (or another visa), which allows long-term stay with the possibility of naturalization. Without CP or approved visa status (T or otherwise), individuals are detained and processed for deportation.

States, with the funding made available from the VTVPA, are also increasingly looking at trafficking as issues of local legislative concern. A number of state and local governments have passed their own antitrafficking laws and ordinances. In addition, local police departments and nonprofit organizations continue to be successful in winning grants for training and programming to combat trafficking and aid victims. These grants are one aspect of the antitrafficking activities enabled through VTVPA funds that look to find victims and traffickers assumed to be otherwise hidden from view. To this end, the Department of State has provided resources to "identify and help trafficking victims" by "looking beneath the surface" (the name of one Department of Heath and Human Services antitrafficking campaign), which includes a list of questions to ask potential victims as well as "indicators [that] flag potential victims." These indicators suggest that the underlying assumptions informing trafficking discourse are that victims show signs of physical and emotional abuse, including bruising or signs of depression, that they are nonnative English speaking or cannot speak "on [their] own behalf," and that they lack documentation like a passport.[44]

Making claim to the category of trafficking victim is by no means an easy process, in part due to the paperwork and, until 2008, the hefty cost necessary for filing this paperwork ($340 in 2007).[45] As scholars like Wendy Chapkis, Julia O'Connell Davidson, Jo Doezema, Dina Francesca Haynes, and Kamala Kempadoo argue, existing legal mechanisms restrict rather than expand definitions of trafficking victimization.[46] Laws like the VTVPA apply a forced or free, worthy or unworthy dichotomy that is characteristic of the history of sexual violence laws in the United States.[47] The consent of victims operates as the key distinguishing feature separating sex slaves from prostitutes and trafficking victims from illegal aliens. The VTVPA implicitly posits the trafficking victim, who lacks consent, against the criminalized sex worker or undocumented migrant. Such a move not only upholds a moralizing framework where sexual virtue is judged as a primary indicator determining whether an individual is deserving of future citizenship, but it simplifies both categories. In the first instance, the law recalls earlier examples from immigration law that equated visual and physical cues with sexual deviancy, where medical, biographical, and visual data were compiled to prove "a distinct prostitute physiognomy" that claimed "the faces of prostitutes looked more degenerate and more mannish, and their genitalia became visibly altered."[48] Such practices are problematic in that they naturalize a link between moral virtue (inner capacity) and the physical body (exterior expression). This is the kind of logic that justified racist practices at the border and elsewhere, as well as racist ideologies like those behind eugenics. In the second instance, the dichotomizing of the trafficking victim against the prostitute or illegal alien assumes that consent can be easily identified and that the categories are mutually exclusive, establishing "a system that celebrates the mobility of capital and some bodies, while the bodies of others face ever-growing restrictions and criminalization."[49]

One of the ways that law and government antitrafficking activities negotiate the tension between the historically exclusionary tendencies of immigration law and the historically abolitionist bent of prostitution laws is to insist on trafficking victims as subjects of repatriation who desire return to countries of origin. Even while reauthorizations of the law take pains to point out domestic trafficking as a potential activity that needs equal attention, trafficking across national borders remains the focus of most government-sponsored antitrafficking activities. For example, one major part of the Department of State's services include the Return, Reintegration, and Family Reunification Program for Victims of Trafficking, established in 2005, which provides "for trafficked persons who elect to return to their home countries . . . safe return and reintegration assistance . . . [which] may include pre-departure assistance, travel documentation, transportation, reception, temporary shelter, health care, training and education, and small grants for income-generating activities."[50] Thus, in cases involving nonnationals, the line between sex worker and trafficking victim is often blurred, where even when victims identify to the contrary, as in Petrova's case, they are nonetheless read as trafficking victims. In this way, the question "who is a prostitute" and the criminalizing of sex work also informs the parameters of antitrafficking law.[51] The premise on which this program of the Department of State rests is one where prostitutes are assumed as more likely to be domestically born, while trafficking victims are more likely to be nonnationals, where part of the violence of trafficking stems precisely from the forcible crossing of national borders. This assumption does more than hide domestic trafficking activities; it helps to construct a national narrative of progress toward greater pluralism and therefore emancipation (explored in chapter 5).

The fact that antitrafficking policy in the United States focuses on repatriation also has the impact of "discouraging [some] women's mobility" and "conveying a simple message: to keep the 'native' at home."[52] Ultimately, the VTVPA has two competing interests, one that is framed through human rights and one that privileges the control of borders, evident in the effort of the U.S. state to maintain distinctions between smuggled individuals who break the law and trafficked victims who do not. While tightening border control is acknowledged as one method of tracking and discouraging trafficking by narrowing the avenues through which people can legally migrate, the tightening of borders ironically leads to greater numbers of undocumented migrants who are more vulnerable to abuse and trafficking conditions because they fall outside the purview of the law.[53]

As an issue tied to immigration and potential citizenry, sex trafficking plays on the anxieties and fears of who reproduces the national body. While the anxieties of opening up immigration through human rights–oriented laws like the VTVPA can be used to understand the need for a process of authentication and the need to distinguish the worthy from the unworthy, the moral premises upon which authentication rests deploy a troubling "politics of virtue," where help is not "freely given; there must be, it is argued, some evidence that those receiving help are in fact deserving of help."[54] Further, the particular focus on trafficking for sex and the ways in which sex trafficked victims are distinguished from sex workers demonstrates the continued state investment in imagining (potential) citizenry through moral frameworks that define "good moral character" through heteronormative, patriarchal, and racialized ideals of female sexuality.

Gendering Expectations, Privileging Speech

Creating a profile of potential victims predisposes law enforcement, government officials, and social service providers to see some bodies as more likely to be potential victims than others. As such, potential victims must selectively navigate which testimonies they use to demonstrate their victimization, largely aware that this may be the only opportunity to participate in the determination of their future legal status. Potential victims of trafficking are often given only a single interview in which they must prove to authenticating officials that they are indeed victims. Many tailor their stories to appeal to what authorities expect to hear so that their victimization should take precedence over their status as undocumented or their status as sexually and morally suspect.

Several early trafficking prosecution cases provide insight into the kinds of assumptions around victimization that are expected and naturalized as markers of trafficking, establishing a link between narrativity and violence.[55] For example, in *United States v. Rosales-Martinez,* Immigration and Customs Enforcement officials raided a New Jersey apartment complex and initially detained thirty female Honduran nationals. According to court records, the Honduran nationals were promised employment in restaurants but forced into sex work in order to repay a $15,000 transportation fee. Of all the initial detainees, federal officials determined that only ten of the women were genuine victims of sex trafficking. The other twenty detainees were processed for deportation. One of the authenticated women was deemed a victim on the basis of testimony that she was "forced to ingest pills designed to induce a spontaneous abortion" and on the following day "had given birth to a live, female infant who died shortly thereafter."[56] Such statements, in playing to both the horrific imagery of abuse as well as antiabortion sentiments that might play well to particular political audiences, demonstrate the desire to cast victims as incapable of helping themselves, justifying "rescue" by U.S. authorities as a moral imperative.[57]

Key physical indicators like size and age are often used in enforcement and legal proceedings to prove that victims are incapable of helping themselves. The case *United States v. Babaev* involved three women who traveled from Azerbaijan to the United States. According to court records, upon arrival in New York, the women were told that they each owed more than $24,000 in fees and were allegedly forced to prostitute themselves in Brooklyn massage parlors to repay the debt. During court proceedings, federal prosecutors stated:

The Third Victim was a vulnerable victim based not only on her age, but on her diminutive physical stature . . . and extreme emotional vulnerability; . . . she is very childlike in her demeanor, manner, and thought process. She is approximately 5 feet tall, and weighs around 100 pounds. On the numerous occasions that the victim was subjected to physical and sexual abuse by [the trafficker] . . . she was physically unable to defend herself.[58]

The prosecutor conflates the physicality of the Third Victim with psychological development where the Third Victim's "emotional vulnerability" is linked to her "diminutive physical stature," used as evidence of her victim status. This linking of "demeanor, manner, and thought process" is troubling insofar as it recalls a "paradigm [that] found expression in the various strands of 'scientific' studies of 'race,' as well as in sexology and criminology,"[59] where the physical body was assumed to be a reliable indicator of intellectual capacity and psychological comportment. Further, the description of the Third Victim, who was seventeen years old at the time of trafficking, as "childlike" not only "coupl[ed] vulnerability with the female gender and dependent children," thereby providing "very potent imagery for the construction of worthy victims,"[60] but it also reinforced gendered constructions of femininity as dependent.

Victim status is thus tied to the successful construction of claimants as incapable of helping themselves, whether due to physical stature, infantile thought process, and/or cultural culpability, as chapter 3 explores. Thus many "anti-trafficking initiatives are infantilizing women, especially third world women, who are regarded as lacking the capacity to reason or choose."[61] While this construction of the victim as incapable of exercising agency is initially necessary in the legal procedure to authenticate victims, this construction enables a teleology of subjecthood that works from silent victim to speaking agent, where agency is exclusively tied to both choice and speech. While the "emphasis on agency is certainly preferable to the paternalistic portrayals of passive victims," Michelle McKinley points to the limits of such a dichotomous victim–agent framework applied "especially in situations of structural violence," where agency is linked to dissent and exit so as to ignore "strategic uses of victimhood narratives" by victims who "frame their experiences in the agreed-upon script to gain [legal recognition]."[62]

The configuring of agency as linked and demonstrated through the enactment of self-aware choice and self-representation through speech is rooted in liberal, post-Enlightenment constructions of the political subject as both self-conscious and rational, where freedom is tied to the (mind's rational) ability to choose. Thus in characterizing victims in antitrafficking legal cases as initially unable to exercise choice, whether due to physical stature, mental incapacity, and/or cultural or economic conditions, the legal process creates a teleological trajectory defining authentic victims as moving from silence and victimhood to (court) testimony and agency. This rather reductive notion of agency implicit in the legal structuring of authenticating trafficking subjects fails to consider the ways agency is a negotiation, "a capacity for action that specific relations of subordination create and enable."[63]

The process of authenticating victims is layered onto this trajectory, where courtroom testimonies offer the venue for victims like Petrova and Third Victim to tell their stories and reclaim their voices, though neglecting consideration of the way their voices "are discursively legitimate only to the extent that they address [expected] issues."[64] The Department of State Office to Monitor and Combat Trafficking's *Trafficking in Persons Report* links this reclamation of speech to justice:

Cooperation of victims cannot be bought or forced, but through the consistent provision of assistance that is not tied to performance in court, victims assured of their rights regain the confidence to speak out for themselves. When this balance is struck effectively, everyone wins—the state, the victim, and society—as a victim finds his or her voice and an exploiter is rendered speechless as justice is handed down.[65]

Acknowledging the potential controversy of requiring authenticated victims to testify in any legal cases brought against traffickers, especially in light of legal scholarship and advocacy tied to the harm that can ensue when survivors of violence are forced to confront those responsible for inflicting harm in often unfriendly courtroom settings, the Department of State report nonetheless links justice for victims to their self-actualization as speaking subjects, where testimonies offer potential legal evidence in trafficking cases. Such self-actualization is enabled here through state mechanisms that bestow onto (worthy) victims both assistance and rights.

While the ability to tell one's story is an incredibly important exercise, it is also one that is not transparent or freely given. Rather, telling one's story and reclaiming one's voice, even freely, is an act embedded in discursive conditions, from the language and imagery available to speakers for articulating their narratives to the existing paradigms and preconceptions through which listeners comprehend the narratives being told. As Gayatri Spivak explains, the act of speech itself already produces the subaltern as a subject effect—an "other" of the (assumed) subject. Thus the very act of naming the subaltern produces her as a subject under the discursive conditions set forth by the conceptual and ideological mechanisms taken for granted in the effort to represent. The position that beings with "the oppressed can know and speak for themselves . . . reintroduces the constitutive subject on at least two levels: the Subject of desire and power as an irreducible methodological presupposition; and the self-proximate, if not self-identical, subject of the oppressed."[66] The constitutive subject is precisely that subject assumed in the post-Enlightenment philosophical texts, which framed subjectivity through desire and power signified through a subject effect ("other" or subject of the oppressed). The very conceptual mechanisms (including the grammatological) through which representation is sought must therefore also be deconstructed.

Speech, like agency, is contingent, and the "evidence of experience" is limited in its conceptual need to assume a subject who preexists discourse rather than allow for the understanding of subjects as shaped with and through discourse.[67] In other words, testimonies and self-speech should not simply be taken as truth statements because "the evidence of experience, whether conceived through a metaphor of visibility or in any other way that takes meaning as transparent, reproduces, rather than contests given ideological systems."[68] When the mostly third world, mostly female trafficked subjects speak to their experiences, their inclusion in the dialogue can simply reify existing paradigms of third world backwardness, a move that in fact imposes another form of violence on such subjects. Agency and testimony must therefore be understood as a negotiation more than as a transparent act; it is never "power-free" or "without interference by entrenched presumptions, sensitivities and preconceived ideas."[69] Yet the conditions tied to claiming victim status hinge on the assumption that speech is transparent and that it is a fundamental marker of the meting out of justice.

While including and recognizing the trafficked subject through the acceptance of her act of self-speech is an invaluable tool for addressing some of the violence inflicted through trafficking, understanding the conditions tied to representation and the circumscribing of speech within broader discursive conditions is key to ensuring that the act of inclusion does not simply serve as an alibi for questions into the uneven relationships of power continuing to inform the writing of global politics and human difference. Eva Petrova's case thus provides a telling voice where the limits of uncritical inclusion are laid bare: Petrova failed in her attempt to speak against the story of victimization imposed on her. Even if she had not opted to leave the United States, and even if she had sought and won permanent legal status, whether that is adequate redress, whether *redress* is even the term under which to understand the violence of trafficking, and whether the United States should reenvision what justice might mean for trafficked subjects are questions to which trafficked subjects like Petrova are never asked to comment. In Petrova's case, one might consider the significance of her decision not to testify in court.

What Petrova's case offers is an opportunity to examine the ways subjectivity is shaped through the interplay of various citational acts. Agency is thus not simply the ability to choose; rather, it is "the double-movement of being constituted in and by a signifier."[70] In the example of trafficking discourses, the agency of trafficked subjects can be found not in their enactment of positive rights or their choice, but in multiple mechanisms through which the scripts and narratives of trafficking are written and rewritten, told and retold. Trafficking subjects are trafficking subjects not only because of their experiences, but because their experiences are recognizable as trafficking violences. These violences are made recognizable through a discursive and representational negotiation between expectations, testimonies, and validations.

Thus when trafficked subjects like Petrova testify to their experiences, they do more than validate or reject existing expectations and definitions of victimization and violence. They help produce and reproduce the boundaries of their subjectivity. After all, as Avery Gordon states, "The stories people tell about themselves, about their troubles, about their social worlds and about their society's problems are entangled and weave between what is immediately available as a story and what their imaginations are reaching toward."[71] It is this weaving that can provide a strategy for reconsidering the productive power of signification and representation that help shape the parameters of how people may exist. The act of self-speech can offer the possibility of exposing the tensions, contradictions, and effacements that take place in the work of producing trafficked subjects as victims. Thus the testimonies offered by women like Petrova offer the possibility of exposing the limits and boundaries of human rights and antitrafficking mechanisms if such testimonies are considered as negotiating a broader field of discourse.

3. Front-Page News

Writing Stories of Victimization and Rescue

The house at 1212½ West Front Street in Plainfield, NJ, is a conventional midcentury home with slate-gray siding, white trim and Victorian lines. When I stood in front of it on a breezy day in October, I could hear the cries of children from the playground of an elementary school around the corner. American flags fluttered from porches and windows. The neighborhood is leafy, middle-class Anytown.

—Peter Landesman, "The Girls Next Door," *New York Times,*
January 25, 2004

SEX TRAFFICKING cases are front-page news, and the ways in which accounts of trafficking are narrated both by news media and government sources shows the discursive and political investment in certain ways of seeing human rights and certain ways of understanding violence, victimization, and agency. The pervasiveness of journalistic accounts similar to the one provided in Peter Landesman's *New York Times* series, where the conventionality of Anytowns like aptly named Plainfield hide a grisly underworld of trafficking, demonstrates how particular narrative tropes are taken for granted and naturalize the relationship between narrative and violence, where violence is only recognizable as such because of its narrative markers. These news stories work with legal scripts to establish dominant cultural narratives of sex trafficking that naturalize gendered notions of citizenship and human rights enactment.

Rather than take for granted these stories of trafficking violence, this chapter considers the pervasiveness of certain kinds of narratives in both the media and state documents as providing an opportunity to explore different kinds of questions into the naturalizing of certain forms of violence with particular narratives and tropes. As Charles Briggs suggests, the questions that need to be asked are, "How do we judge a narrative as being 'about' a particular event? What gives us the feeling that it 'captures' what 'really happened'? . . . How can acts of violence and acts of narration be brought into such an intimate relationship that stories can be read as forms whose features provide a reliable way of knowing acts that are hidden from us—and whose reality we accept by virtue of their indexical connection to an act of narration?"[1] Identifying narrative indexes that come to shape the sex trafficking story, as well as tropes like the American Dream through which such stories are refracted, can illustrate the ways the rescuer and victim are distinguished through the notion of the ethics and culture of (legitimate, capitalist) work, which enables the valoration of (neo)liberal principles.

Taking such effects as a narrative violence, this chapter traces the story of sex trafficking as told through mainstream media outlets like the *New York Times* and the *San Francisco Chronicle*, both newspapers that have run special series on sex trafficking. Additionally, news media sources like PBS and MSNBC as well as books authored by journalists identifying the narrative conventions that mark the story as about sex trafficking are the focus of this chapter, which suggests that the sex trafficking story reveals more about the national subject invested in finding victims ready for rescue than anything else. The storytelling conventions demonstrated in journalistic accounts of sex trafficking are important not because they help reveal a hidden truth about trafficking, but because they, along with state documents, explain trafficking through cultural arguments that reaffirm the need for outside rescue, reducing human rights to the differential valuation of bodies and naturalizing constructions of the "backwardness" of culpable cultures. Media pieces work alongside state documents and NGO literature and research to produce a discourse of trafficking, where "the strategies of women's human rights advocates . . . resonated with a set of conventionalized journalistic images and associations."[2]

Constructing Intimacies in the Journey to Uncover Hidden Truths

In his opening paragraph, Landesman introduces David Miranda, a cashier working in the neighborhood's local convenience store, who describes the suspect comings and goings of the otherwise conventional home at 1212½ West Front Street:

David Miranda, the young man behind the counter of Westside Convenience, told me he saw girls from the house roughly once a week. "They came in to buy candy and soda, then went back to the house," he said. The same girls rarely came twice, and they were all very young, Miranda said. They never asked for anything beyond what they were purchasing; they certainly never asked for help. Cars drove up to the house all day; nice cars, all kinds of cars. Dozens of men came and went. "But no one here knew what was really going on," Miranda said. And no one ever asked.[3]

While Miranda notes that he rang up purchases made by different girls coming from the house, it is Landesman who directs the reader to the suspect aspect of what Miranda has observed. Situating himself as the one who knows better—who knows better than to accept the fact that "no one ever asked" about the suspicious cars and men coming and going from the house—Landesman's piece exemplifies a trend in media pieces on sex trafficking where the journalist plays a key role in the narrative of sex trafficking. Readers identify with Landesman and his keen eye, even while readers might also identify with Miranda, who sees the signs but does not yet know—or simply chooses to ignore—their significance. Miranda is ultimately cast as foil to Landesman, who emerges as one of the heroes of his own story by helping to uncover the hidden activities of trafficking.

Beginnings situated in a seemingly conventional setting where trafficking exists as hidden and journalists who take an active role in the unfolding of a rescue narrative provide recurring indexes through which news stories frame their recognizability as stories about sex trafficking. In doing so, they "transform mere happenings into publically discussable events."[4] These stories are also recognizable in their foreign beginnings (Korea, Eastern Europe, Latin America, and so on),[5] where nonnationals play the central role of victim even though trafficking need not cross national borders or involve nonnational players. Rarely do sex trafficking news items implicate domestic-born U.S. citizens as victims. When they do, the stories tend to identify these domestic victims as underage girls and runaways who are usually white and come from conventional middle-class backgrounds.[6] An emblematic example of the treatment of domestic trafficking can be found in *New York Times* op-ed columnist Nicholas Kristof's writing on sex trafficking, where he briefly mentions the "white, middle-class blonde [who] goes missing," but only to draw a contrast to the thousands of Asian women who are kidnapped and trafficked. The story of sex trafficking that implicates runaway suburban teens seems to be less compelling (if this is measured by frequency), and it is certainly less prominent than the stories told about immigrant victims.[7] The recurring conventions found in news stories of sex trafficking are important because "news stories achieve their powerful indexical iconicity by framing themselves as verbal photographs, if you will, telling the story of their own production in such a way as to prove that they were produced through the very actions that produced the crime story, which itself was produced by the material and verbal traces of the crime."[8]

The wedding of the journalistic exposé with the rescue narrative, where the journalist becomes a key player enabling the unfolding of the story, is a crucial index of the story of sex trafficking. For example, in the PBS *Frontline* television special "Sex Slaves," the journalist's harrowing ethical dilemma resulting from his inability to distance himself from the story is combined with the rescue narrative of one husband searching for his wife sold into sex slavery.[9] "Sex Slaves" combines the drama of Viorel's search for his wife, Katia, who was unknowingly sold into slavery when Katia traveled to Turkey, with the reporting crew's own dramatic journey to uncover sex trafficking in Ukraine and Moldova while helping Viorel rescue Katia. Sex trafficking stories are recognizable as such in part because of their beginnings, where the hidden dangers and truths of trafficking implicate innocent victims like Katia, brutalized by her traffickers and left to disappear unless rescued. In these stories, the rescue of victims is enabled through the intervention of the journalists, who either directly rescue the victim or aid a proxy like Viorel.[10]

"Sex Slaves" demonstrates the way news stories of trafficking depart from conventional strategies that mark objective journalistic reporting. While conventional news reporting rests on the establishment of authority through various strategies indicating objectivity, including the seeming emotional distance between the reporter and story,[11] it is precisely the inability of journalists to remain emotionally uninvolved that gives sex trafficking news stories their authority. For example, "Sex Slaves" uses an unseen narrator to explain the facts about trafficking and frame the action taking place in the news piece. Yet as the piece unfolds, the film crew becomes more and more involved with Viorel in his plan to pretend to be a pimp looking for Katia. The story documents the producers as they provide Viorel with a hidden camera. When Viorel's initial interaction with Katia's captor goes sour, leading to the severing of contact between Viorel and the woman he believes is keeping his wife, the cameras follow Viorel's desperate attempts to have producer Felix Golubev pose as an Interpol agent and confront Viorel's liaison about the illegal activity she admits to on the hidden recording. Here the story shifts to focus on the journalists' ethical dilemma:

> NARRATOR: Viorel's plan has put the production team in an ethical bind.
>
> RIC ESTHER BIENSTOCK [producer]: I don't know if we're crossing a line. What do you guys think?
>
> FELIX GOLUBEV: He's not exactly a rational guy, at this point. He's desperate. He wants to threaten them. He thinks it's going to work.
>
> RIC ESTHER BIENSTOCK: Frankly, I think there's more of a danger that if they see that, what's the point of giving up his wife? They'll just can hurt her [*sic*]. . . . I'm just worried that he puts himself in more danger and that he ends up getting the crap beaten out of him, if not worse, and that we end up being responsible for that because we provided the materials for that.[12]

The story's voice-over narration inserts the two producers' debate over the pros and cons of having one of the film crew pose as an Interpol agent into the narrative of Katia and Viorel. While Golubev decides not to concede to Viorel's request, maintaining his position as separate from his story and subjects, Golubev's behind-the-scenes conversation with the production crew nonetheless becomes part of the story. This revelatory moment—the exchange and the fact that it plays a significant part in the unfolding drama of Viorel's rescue and Katia's victimization—also works to establish the journalist's credibility as an ethical and compassionate player, an outsider who is central to the eventual rescue of both Katia and Viorel. Intimacy is established not only between viewer/reader and journalist, but between the journalist and his or her story. Unlike conventional news reporting, the narrative of trafficking is one where the journalists' inability to stay above the story works to provide credibility to both.

News stories are, after all, stories, with settings, plot development, and central characters. Stories of sex trafficking are appealing in part because of the inherent human drama and seemingly clear-cut moral characters—victims and criminals. Stories of sex trafficking thus strongly demonstrate that "the U.S. news narrative is descended from the quintessential American art form, the western,"[13] where the mythical line between so-called objective news reporting and sensationalist tabloid stories is blurred.[14] While serious news outlets in the United States (and also Britain) demonstrate more closely what Daniel Hallin and Paolo Mancini describe as the liberal model, where commercial presses developed with little relative state involvement, leading to a tradition of seemingly politically neutral reporting,[15] they and other media scholars point out the ways traditional news outlets are more editorial than they may seem at first glance.[16] Stories of sex trafficking are recognizable as such in part because of the way they have been reported and narrated, even in serious news outlets like the *New York Times,* through first-person accounts that often explicitly recount the journalist's decision to abandon journalistic conventions of neutral reporting at some point in the plot's unfolding.

While in the *Frontline* report the crew decides to remain objective observers of the story, in many other accounts journalists choose to pose as potential solicitors or johns in their search for the hidden activities and victims of sex trafficking, a move that places the journalist as a character within the narrative of the news story. These accounts of sex trafficking often elicit an intimacy with the reader, which is posed implicitly against the false intimacy implied in the relationship between the sex-trafficked victim and the john. This strategy of the undercover journalist not only directly inserts and implicates the reporter into the story, it also allows the story itself to convey an intimacy between journalist/undercover john and his subject/trafficking victim, which both becomes an index of legitimacy and suggests that the lack of intimacy and compassion of real johns toward victims is an integral part of the problem.

Any potential question into the validity of the reporting, especially on an issue that the news stories themselves represent as underground and hidden, is answered through the strategy of posing as undercover players or even the abandoned yet contemplated discussion of going undercover (as in the case of the *Frontline* report). A tactic employed by male journalists like Nicholas Kristof of the *New York Times,* Canadian journalist and author of *The Natashas* Victor Malarek, and the production team of MSNBC's *Undercover: Sex Slaves in America,* posing as johns to gain access to the otherwise hidden world of sex trafficking also frames the story as one of rescue, where a secondary rescuer like Viorel or other sympathetic players like the police are ultimately overshadowed by primary rescuers initially seemingly outside the action and emotion of the story. The fact that the journalist is unable to keep him- or herself outside the story works as an indicator of both the story and the journalist's credibility. The impact of linking the story's credibility to the journalist's inability to stay objective and outside the story rests on the description of sex trafficking as a crime so abhorrent that anyone doing "real" reporting would feel compelled to intervene.

The reporter/researcher unable to keep from becoming involved has become an indexical icon of the sex trafficking story even when the stories are not told by journalists. For example, former investment banker and board member of the NGO Free the Slaves, Siddharth Kara's 2009 book *Sex Trafficking: Inside the Business of Modern Slavery* finds the author recounting his various experiences in brothels in India, Italy, Thailand, and the United States, where posing as a john enables Kara to solicit interviews with women he suspects are trafficking victims (though the women never self-identify as such). In his book, Kara is the central protagonist, and in part because there is no claim to journalistic objectivity, his narrative is written in a more explicit personal manner, where readers are told of Kara's thoughts and emotions even as he describes being part of the action. For instance, when describing an attempt to discover sex trafficking victims by posing as a john, Kara states, "I felt anxious. If anything went wrong, I could not speak Italian and I was far away from urban safety." The subsequent encounter with a Lithuanian teenager who Kara "figure[s] . . . had not traveled willingly" based on her age, is almost an afterthought to Kara's own anxiety and attempt to provide the teenager with a phone number for assistance.[17] While not a formally trained journalist, Kara's Columbia University Press video promoting the book presents Kara reporting on his book in a manner reminiscent of television news, on-location reporting.[18] Close-ups of Kara, dressed in a suit jacket and narrating about sex trafficking, are intertwined with stock footage of the book's cover and images of various brown bodies depicting life in an unnamed third world locale (marked as such by visual cues—brown bodies, distinctive architecture). What is left unexamined in narratives where storytellers go undercover are the ways such practices, by constructing an "ethical john,"[19] implicitly remove responsibility from johns as participants in trafficking's violence.

The construction of an ethical john can take many shapes: an undercover reporter simply looking to interview otherwise hidden victims of sex trafficking, or a john turned boyfriend who is a character in the story.[20] In the latter case, johns become boyfriends or reformed citizens in order to provide the story with a proxy rescuer, a move that implicitly affirms the construction of "good" sex as uncommodified and freely given. The ethical john is both explicitly and implicitly contrasted to the bad john, whose desire to commodify sex is what characterizes him as bad. In the final installment of a special front-page, four-part series on sex trafficking that ran in 2006 in the *San Francisco Chronicle,* one victim, You Mi Kim, meets a "28-year-old man, who had weaved in from a nearby bar where he was drinking away a bad breakup . . . who didn't grab at her."[21] This description is in contrast to the bad johns who bring "pornographic magazines to show You Mi what they wanted her to do."[22] The ethical john takes Kim out on dates and eventually helps Kim make the decision to leave sex work: "He took her to the Golden Gate Bridge and Baker Bridge, and bought her first pair of hiking shoes."[23] Rather than present this ethical john as also complicit in the purchasing of sex, his initial desire to buy sex is cast through a compassionate light, where his momentary lapse in morals is explained through a bad breakup and a night of drinking. Similarly, his purchasing of gifts is cast as an innocent act of giving, rather than part of an exchange of goods and services.

Though this ethical john plays a part in ending Kim's story by helping to free her from her decision to remain in sex work, it is Meredith May's reporting that draws attention to the fact that Kim's decision to remain in sex work was not really a decision at all, but a form of sex trafficking's violence. The series ends with May quoting Kim: "'Most customers come into a massage parlor thinking nothing is wrong; that it's a job we choose,' she said. 'It doesn't occur to them that we are slaves.'"[24] It is May who elicits this statement from Kim, suggesting that the journalist's insistence over her ten-month interview period is integral to helping Kim arrive at seeing the truth—seeing the markers of sex trafficking and being able to know better. May's narrative thus not only inserts the reporter as a central figure in Kim's story, but also allows readers to see what they might otherwise never suspect by helping to establish "narratives [that] enable us to grasp an object that, unless we witness or participate in the violence, we do not know directly."[25]

While male journalists can go undercover as johns, female journalists like *San Francisco Chronicle's* May are able to establish credibility through the implication that women who are sex trafficking victims are more willing and more honest in speaking to other women. While the strategy of posing undercover plays on a sense of intimacy between male journalists and his subjects and story, and thus intimacy with his reader, female journalists often play on sentiments of global sisterhood to elicit intimacy and credibility. In May's *San Francisco Chronicle* series, intimacy is further constructed through the title, "Diary of a Sex Slave." This narrative plays on the rhetorically constructed intimacy between female journalist and source, where May provides the private diary details of Kim's ordeal. The notion that women are more likely to share secrets with other women draws on the assumption of evidentiary experience as a way to validate truths, where the experience of being women provides evidence of the fact of that shared difference.[26]

The notion that female trafficked subjects are more likely to feel at ease with female journalists reaffirms the idea of an unnamed universality to simply being women. The prohibitionist NGO Coalition Against Trafficking in Women offers a "Press for Change" guide for journalists reporting on sex trafficking. Authored by Julie Bindel, a freelance journalist who often writes for (London's) *Guardian,* the guide includes a "do" and "don't" list, which states the importance of "try[ing] to ensure that female interviewees are interviewed by women."[27] At the risk of simplifying the circumstances of different women who find themselves trafficked subjects, such a blanket assumption fails to consider that in some cases those inflicting harm may also be women, that women victims may not necessarily be more comfortable speaking to women reporters, or that female victims may not necessarily see their female-ness as a primary way of identifying.

The discovery and revelation of the narrative of sex trafficking posits the journalist as rescuer and suggests that it is the revelation itself that can act as a solution to the violence of sex trafficking.[28] Such revelations are also posited as the result of the journalist's hard work, where journalists caution against accepting interviews from victims too quickly and emphasize that real victims are often reluctant to share their stories.[29] The theme of hard work—hard work of the journalists, the proxy rescuers of the story, and the victims—also serves as an indexical icon of the sex trafficking story. This marker, however, does more than make the story recognizable as a sex trafficking narrative uncovering hidden "truths"; it also instills national narratives that help define values tied to "being Americans."

Principles of individualism and the Protestant work ethic help shape the narrative core of the story in a manner that ultimately saddles the blame for trafficking on "native" cultures. Thus the violence of sex trafficking exists not just in the reported abduction, coercion, rape, and abuse of trafficked subjects, but also in the way the narrativizing of sex trafficking's violence affirms developmental progress frames that pit "backward" cultures against the progress of human rights.

Cultural Culprits and Dreams Deferred

The narrative landscape of sex trafficking defines the activity through the scope of rescue and the uncovering of hidden activities, whether this is recounted through raids on suspect brothels, stories of ethical johns, or tales chronicling journalistic ethics. These stories focus on the moral dilemmas of (ethical) johns, journalists, police, and the reading public where there is little ambiguity in separating good actors from criminal traffickers. The moral frame helps to construct cultures of complicity that resonate with existing notions of third world backwardness and U.S. progressiveness, which also frame some political development theories. Thus these stories end up providing indexical icons of the violence and criminal activities of sex trafficking as well as indexical icons of the national character.

These stories reflect, refract, and shape notions of national identity and character, evident in the ways the rhetoric of the American Dream works as an organizing frame in the story's attempt to explain trafficking. Just as May begins her "Diary of a Sex Slave" with You Mi Kim's credit card debt and *Frontline* explains Katia's trip to Turkey without her husband to be a result of economic necessity, the story of sex trafficking is driven by what the U.S. Department of State describes as "women eager for a better future" who are "susceptible to the promises of jobs abroad as babysitters, housekeepers, waitresses, or models—

jobs that traffickers turn into the nightmare of prostitution without exit."[30] In May's piece, Kim's initial desire for the American Dream puts her in so much debt that she decides to answer an ad to "work in an American room salon. Make $10,000 a month."[31]

Writing to demonstrate Kim's initial desire to participate (correctly) in the spirit of capitalism and the Protestant work ethic, May emphasizes the lack of economic opportunities for women in South Korea. The first segment of "Diary" is titled "A Youthful Mistake" and runs with the line, "You Mi Kim was a typical college student, until her first credit card got her into trouble." The segment introduces Kim as "the perfect victim: a small-town girl in financial trouble" who doesn't know any better.[32] Kim is represented as youthfully innocent and gullible, where gendered images of vulnerability evident in state documents and legal testimonies also circulate in news stories: "A friend explained to You Mi that she could buy things without cash. A magic card, You Mi thought."[33] Kim is redeemable precisely because she initially quits school to work a legitimate service-sector job. When this option shows no sign of helping her earn enough to begin paying off her debt, she contemplates "the unthinkable: sell her body," but she ultimately decides "she couldn't stomach the thought of having sex with strangers for money."[34] She then answers the call for work in the United States as a kind of waitress, which promises that the job does not include prostitution and pays significantly more than what she is making in South Korea. Thus Kim's decision to immigrate comes from a morally recognizable desire to work for "a better future" in a job characterized as within the morally acceptable confines of babysitting, housekeeping, waitressing, or modeling—work that ironically often falls under the radar of the formal economy in ways similar to the sex industry.

Recalling familiar narratives of the American Dream where the promise of a better life abroad begins the tale of hard work, challenge, and eventual success, these stories present sex trafficking as a perversion and therefore a threat to this U.S.-American sense of identity. While traffickers are clear-cut criminals and antagonists, the fact that Kim falls into credit card debit because of her failure to apprehend principles of thrift—a central tenet of the spirit of capitalism—despite her college education casts a culture of culpability linked to Kim's difference from May and her U.S. reader counterpart.

The significance of cultural culpability in trafficking is also evident in state documents, many of which reproduce sex trafficking narratives that highlight individual victims in a manner very similar to media pieces. For instance, even while economic conditions are noted as the primary reason why women find themselves victims of sex trafficking, the moral of these stories suggests that economic conditions can be overcome with the right kind of values or exacerbated with the wrong values. This rendering of economic conditions as a backdrop for questions of whether an individual has the right set of (cultural) values or is able to learn these values unimpeded by bad cultural culprits and traffickers naturalizes economic inequality as something that is unalterable. This can be seen, for instance, in the State Department's annual *Trafficking in Persons Report* from 2003:

Greed and the widespread subjugation of women in much of the world facilitate trafficking. Poor countries have been flooded with images of wealth and prosperity beamed in through television or radio and lavish displays of wealth send powerful messages to impoverished citizens about the benefits of material acquisition. More often than not, an "ends justifies the means" rationale has taken root within communities to legitimize the source of the wealth, regardless of how acquired.[35]

Here the Department of State identifies greed and patriarchal attitudes as primary causes of trafficking. The attitudes of peoples of "poor countries" that the "end justifies the means" not only cause trafficking but legitimize it. Similar to the characterization of Kim's inability to grasp the correct values of capitalism, leading her into a shopping spree of "metallic handbags, low-rise jeans, high-heeled boots, skin-care creams, digital cameras and American-style sneakers,"[36] the story of sex trafficking implicates attitudes lacking in hard work and thrift—attitudes that simply covet the acquisition of markers of wealth—as the reason why individuals become victims.

By postponing the question of how some nations come to and remain in relative poverty while others do not, the Department of State makes culture the culprit. The difference of poor countries from wealthy ones is not about the uneven circuits of capital resulting from colonialism and war, but the immoral, greedy, and patriarchal cultural attitudes and practices of the people. Reasserting the view that "capitalism cannot make use of the labour of those who practice the doctrine of undisciplined *liberum arbitrium*, any more than it can make use of the business man who seems absolutely unscrupulous in his dealings with others,"[37] the Department of State's position is one that adheres to a "spirit of capitalism" that distinguishes different modes of acquiring wealth through the assessment of attitudes of hard work.

Furthermore, the lack of "rational capitalistic organization" is not simply a matter of individual lapses but is an indicator that all of the cultural community is culpable.[38] "Bad" attitudes and values are not simply individual problems, but cultural and national ones. For example, in May's piece, she situates Kim's failure to properly apprehend the mechanisms of capitalism to all South Koreans: "Fashion is a major cultural preoccupation for South Koreans. . . . Poverty is considered a mortal sin. Such intense pressure to acquire 'American luxury goods' puts the average South Korean family in $30,000 credit card debt."[39] Further, it is South Korea's lack of "high-paying jobs" for women that May posits as the broader context resulting in Kim's victimization.[40]

Reminiscent of the culture of poverty rhetoric that seeks to explain poverty as an outcome of a way of thinking about money and work that fails to apprehend thrift, savings, and hard work, the narrative of sex trafficking reasserts the idea of culture as key to understanding why sex trafficking originates in certain parts of the globe and with certain people and not others. For instance, in a report prepared for the International Organization for Migration (IOM), sex trafficking in Russia is explained as resulting from "severe economic decline" coupled with "psychological and attitudinal changes of people, especially women" that comes as a result of "images of glamour and wealth from the West by the media."[41] This view of sex trafficking in the Russian Federation reasserts what the Department of State notes a year later—that trafficking results from certain peoples' inability to properly cope with material/economic changes (by either accepting their relative poverty or by participating in legitimate sectors of the capitalist economy). The idea of individual responsibility for "psychological and attitudinal changes" works along with the construction of cultures of culpability to cast the problem of trafficking as about individuals kept from proper values by their cultural communities.

Even when the framing of sex trafficking is attentive to the combination of globalization, militarism, and colonialism all as reasons for trafficking,[42] the suggestion is that these political formations simply exacerbate already present cultural conditions that enable trafficking. In May's piece, the sex industry situated near U.S. military bases "where

Japanese troops built the first brothels after invading the country in 1904" is prefaced with the statement that "the selling of Korean women goes back to the 15th century."[43] Even while colonialism and militarism are implicated in creating conditions for sex trafficking, the narrative situates these conditions within a more entrenched cultural condition. Such a move naturalizes the construction of "originating" and "native" places as always backward in their adherence to cultural practices enabling sex trafficking, despite colonialism, imperialism, and military occupation. Further, the backwardness of culpable cultures is measured through adherence to patriarchy, constructing native places as backward precisely because of their inability to grasp feminist principles.

Globalization and immigration thus become a means through which to explain the resurrection of a backward practice like sex trafficking in more so-called developed regions of the world (namely, the United States and Western Europe).[44] Criminal traffickers and immigrant victims are narrativized as bringing trafficking to the United States and other developed nations. Further, the culture of complicity of those who solicit from traffickers is never implicated in the same ways as the native culture incapable of properly educating victims like Kim to either the spirit of capitalism or proper gender relations. For instance, the fact that there are ethical johns suggests that the culture enabling the illicit soliciting of sex can be overcome, or, as in the case of Kim's boyfriend, is a momentary lapse in an overall progressive national culture. This is in contrast to the construction of the native culture as always having been culpable in the kind of patriarchal relations that today enable sex trafficking.

Attitudes about wealth, poverty, and work—attitudes that collectively create a culture—provide the key reasoning to explain how poverty results in trafficking. This is significant not only in displacing the salience of the (historical) how and why of economic inequality, but also because the idea of cultural culpability enables the naturalizing of "backward others" as also racial others, where backwardness is indicated through visual readings of the body. Culture thus operates as a rhetorical tool that names difference even while hiding the historical production and operation of categories of difference. In other words, while culture often refers to a group of people distinguished by language and tradition, and identifiable through visual or aural apprehension, culture refuses to see how it is tied to the racial terms of difference it hopes to substitute and replace. Culture, when it is understood as a fixed category describing a shared set of behaviors and beliefs that help identify communities, helps to instill a "new bigotry—not of types of people but of ways of being,"[45] which serves as a site of racialization.

Cultural failure to grasp so-called correct means of wealth acquisition is tied to a propensity toward patriarchy, helping to construct native cultures as backward in their relative modernity. This characterization often takes the form of implicating rural cultures and small towns (as in the case of Kim's story). For instance, rural culture, according to Human Rights Watch, dictates family structures and community expectations in places like Southeast Asia, where trafficking is encouraged by cultural assumptions that normalize the selling of daughters:

> Of the 30 girls and women, 11 have been brought into Thailand by family members. The network for finding work in Thailand appears to be well known in the rural areas of Burma that supply the women and girls. Relatives knew, for example, to take their daughters or sisters to the "Mekong shop" in Mae Sai or to a particularly well-known agent or to a certain temple.[46]

The fact that relatives of trafficked victims are characterized as knowing and willing in the commerce of girls and women suggests a deviant culture of patriarchy, one that extends beyond the bad choices of any individual to characterize the culture as a whole. The fact that women are trafficked by their own family members, people who should have the women's best interest in mind, further characterizes the deviancy and moral degeneracy of these (Southeast Asian) cultures—not even the mothers and sisters have the moral capacity to see the selling of family members as abhorrent, and even if they do, they nonetheless participate in the activity out of economic desperation. Thus, the solution to trafficking entails teaching women the moral values necessary to see trafficking as a bad activity because their cultural conditions normalize and condone trafficking, even making it an activity in which family members participate. Hence, so long as victims come from the same cultural community as traffickers, outside rescue remains the only solution.

The implication of patriarchy to the cultural culpability of some peoples and nations defines patriarchy as problematic because it keeps women from awareness and self-determination. This construction of patriarchy relies on decidedly liberal definitions of feminism where gender equity is gauged by women's ability to make choices for themselves.

The trafficked woman, insofar as she fails to question the "right of [her] families . . . to sell them,"[47] is not only unable to choose but also unable to see that she has a claim to her own individual rights. She is thus cast as part of the problem: she enables the very culture that sells and traffics her, rendering her rescue from outside imperative. Hence stories of sex trafficking may involve a primary rescuer (a good individual even amid bad cultural conditions) like a husband or understanding john, as in *Frontline's* story of Viorel's rescue attempts. However, there is always also a need for an outside rescuer leaving sex trafficking stories to posit the journalist or storyteller (or in the case of state documents, the concerned citizen or state official) into this role.[48] Native cultures culpable for trafficking are constructed as never giving victims the opportunity of knowing, and thus narratives of rescue like that driving the Department of State's antitrafficking agenda highlight the "'three R's'—rescue, rehabilitation, and reintegration,"[49] where prevention and rehabilitation rest heavily on education—in other words, in correcting the cultural beliefs that render trafficked subjects lacking in awareness of their individual ability to self-determination.[50] Such approaches, while they may be helpful in some circumstances, take for granted and reaffirm the rightness of liberal principles of individualism, where self-betterment out of bad cultural conditions requires the correcting of certain kinds of consciousnesses.

This framing further enables the bifurcating of the globe into human rights–enacting states like the United States and those of Western Europe posed against human rights–violating states characterizing the third world and republics of the former USSR. Sex trafficking is thus narrativized as a matter for concern for the U.S. state and citizens insomuch as trafficking victims and criminal traffickers enter into the United States to run prostitution rings,[51] and the activities of trafficking result in a moral lapse (already existing in the nations of origin and momentary in the destination countries). The problem of sex trafficking is cast as twofold. First is the soliciting and selling of sex, a behavior that can be remedied through a moral appeal, both to the john who solicits and the trafficked woman who sells. Second, the production of the conditions that lead certain women into trafficking that cannot be altered without the prosecution and sometimes eradication of the men who enable and perpetuate these traditions. Furthermore, characterizing traffickers as individual men who are criminal and/or cultures of criminality evident in the implication of Japanese Yakuza, Chinese Triads, the Russian Mafia and corrupt native governments works to ignore the ways corporations, businesses (capitalism's so-called legitimate players), and even law enforcement and the military can participate in and perpetuate trafficking conditions.

The Violence of Modernity: Universalizing Liberal Traditions

Constructing a culture of complicity and culpability is troubling insofar as such a framing poses victims of trafficking as part of the problem. Trafficked subjects are always already victimized by cultural conditions that never enable the possibility of knowing better or the possibility of self-enlightenment without an outside rescuer. These dichotomous framings of victim and rescuer, failing and successful cultures, backward native and modern subject conceptualize cultural communities as closed, static, and hierarchically organized in a teleological progression toward human rights enactment/fulfillment. Thus the narrativizing of sex trafficking inflicts its own violence in establishing conditions of subjectivity—conditions through which trafficking victims, criminals, and rescuers can be understood as such—that reaffirm constructions of first world progress against third world and sometimes second world inability.

In writing the subjects of trafficking in cultural terms, cultural communities are cast as "not yet"—not yet realizing feminist potential, not yet enacting human rights values, not yet as modern or progressive as their Euro-American counterparts (who are placed in the role of rescuer). This writing as not yet recalls a legacy of Enlightenment and post-Enlightenment humanism grounded in principles of liberalism, where humanity is defined by a mechanism of differentiation that writes a "waiting-room version of history," which works by "saying 'not yet' to somebody else."[52] The not yet nonetheless offers the possibility of inclusion—of becoming a human rights–enacting subject or a culture defined by human rights principles. This promise works to universalize liberal principles of humanism that define humanity through rationality, individualism, and self-determination by offering the possibility of including those not yet, whose consciousnesses are clouded by affectability,[53] into modern conditions.

Subjects in the trafficking story are produced through the mechanisms and strategies of post-Enlightenment texts that necessitate an "other" figure to stand against and before the modern subject, making victim status necessarily absolute. These "other" figures are always and already not yet human rights enacting, in opposition to their already human rights–enacting counterparts. The writing of subjects as either "enacting" or "not yet" universalizes an understanding of humanity grounded in modern principles, where subjects are ultimately defined by their exercise of agency and self-consciousness. In liberal terms, this amounts to the individual capacity to choose and implement rights. Making cultures culpable ensures this writing of humanity by leaving some perpetually not yet able to enact human rights as a result of the ways these communities are affected by their cultures despite individual attempts at reform.

Further, it is not only in the reification of troubling dichotomies and stereotypes that the narrativizing of sex trafficking inflicts violence. It is also in the ways the story constructs victim subjectivity as absolute. In May's narrative, for example, when Kim opts to remain in the sex industry even after ties to her traffickers have ceased, she is still characterized as a victim. May writes that five months after being "lured from her home in South Korea by international sex traffickers," Kim was let go. After gaining her freedom, Kim still faced "a $40,000 shopping debt back home" that she decided would be most quickly paid off if she remained in the sex industry: "Any kind of job she could get as an illegal immigrant—cleaning homes or washing dishes in a restaurant—wouldn't pay her debts in time. . . . You Mi felt she had no choice. On her first day of freedom, she took an unlicensed Korean taxi from Los Angeles to another illicit massage parlor in San Francisco."[54] Never quoting Kim, May narrates Kim's choice to remain in the sex industry as never really a choice, or a choice born out of desperation and exacerbated by her trafficking. The reader never actually knows whether "You Mi felt she had no choice."

Even when victims like Kim act as decision makers and exercise what otherwise would be considered self-aware choice, the trafficked subject is nonetheless rendered victimized. Journalist Victor Malarek recounts for *Frontline:* "People have said to me, 'Well these girls can run.' They can't. They're taken to these apartments and these houses, usually in remote areas, and men come in and break them. They make her submit to every indignity in front of all the girls. They beat her and do whatever."[55] While this description of victimization might accurately describe the experiences of some, the way this image of victimization becomes an indexical icon for all trafficking violence is troubling in that it frames victim status as absolute. Even when the writing of victims allows for some agency in choosing to remain in sex work, there is still a general admission that acknowledges the structural confines of patriarchy under which prostitution operates. The question of "which proportion would choose prostitution as an occupation if society had offered them any other reasonable option" underwrites sex trafficking narratives,[56] suggesting that the choice in sex work is ultimately limited by the larger cultural and economic conditions subjugating women.

Given the absoluteness of the ways victims are described in sex trafficking narratives, the desire to see that "women need not always be victims, but can take hold of their own lives, and create a better future for themselves and their community" is an understandable one.[57] However, reading trafficked subjects as decision makers and agents does not necessarily dismantle the operations of power that problematically produce her as not yet, nor does this move question the universalizing of liberal principles and modern epistemologies. The ontological framework through which trafficked subjects are written as not yet remains in place whether the trafficked subject is characterized as victim or agent. This is problematic in that the notion of agency is defined "within the realm of individual action that only regards certain types of actions as agentive and rational. . . . Certain types of action [are] represented as coercion (victimhood) [which] denounces other actions as expressions of false consciousness."[58]

The capacity to read the narrativizing of sex trafficking for the various "cartographies of communication" at work not only exposes the ways "powerful actors . . . determine what will count as silences, lies, and surpluses, just as they create silences of their own,"[59] but it also reveals the assumptions around understanding subjects and being that universalize modern regimes of knowledge. Thus the violence of sex trafficking exists beyond the activities described by state documents and journalists; it also exists in the way such accounts are narrated: "Newspaper stories, like narratives told in courtrooms, police stations, and everyday rumors, raise important issues about how violence gets ideologically separated from the violence of modernity, extracted from history

and political economy, individualized as products of pathological subjectivities and defective domesticities, and made to represent entire populations, thereby naturalizing representations of class, gender, space,
state, and nation."[60]

The violence of modernity can be glimpsed in trafficking narratives
in the writing of victimization as absolute and the casting of culture as
culpable. This is elucidated in Nicholas Kristof's *New York Times* series on
trafficking. Kristof, a Rhodes scholar whose studies in Arabic and Chinese no doubt helped land him beats in Asia, won his second Pulitzer for
what judges called columns "that gave voice to the voiceless in other
parts of the world."[61] Attentiveness to how such voices are framed and
the broader discursive landscape these voices help shape, which in turn
helps produce meanings around human rights, can demonstrate the
ways representational violence characterizes sex trafficking.

Beginning in 2004 and continuing into 2007, the *New York Times*
ran several of his editorial pieces. In an early piece on sex trafficking,
Kristof writes about meeting two girls in Cambodia, Srey Neth and Srey
Mom, whom he decides to "free." Beginning his column with the statement, "One thinks of slavery as an evil confined to musty sepia photographs. But there are 21st-century versions of slaves as well, girls like
Srey Neth," Kristof recounts how he met Srey Neth, who "insisted at first
(through my Khmer interpreter) that she was free and not controlled
by the guesthouse." Noting that Srey Neth "soon told her real story,"
Kristof continues to write about the story of abuse the two girls provide. The column ends with the following exchange between Kristof
and Srey Mom:

> "Do you really want to leave the brothel?" I ask.
> "I love myself," she answered simply. "I do not want to let my life be de-
> stroyed by what I'm doing now."
> That's when I made a firm decision I'd been toying with for some time: I
> would try to buy freedom for these two girls and return them to their families.[62]

Kristof makes a moral assessment—it is only when Srey Mom proves
to Kristof that she recognizes that her life is being destroyed by her
"slavery" that Kristof decides to buy her freedom. The fact that buying
the girl's freedom further commodifies them suggests that this is not
the problem; rather, the problem according to Kristof's account is in the
ways the girls are kept from living lives of their choosing, evidenced in

both girls' eventual acceptance of Kristof's offer of freedom. When Kristof later finds Srey Mom back at her old brothel (this time refusing the interpreter's offer to take her to a women's shelter), he concedes that there are "few fairy-tale endings in sexual trafficking. (I hope the teenager, Srey Neth, will have one, for she has now built a tin-roofed shack and stocked it as a grocery, and is proudly earning a living for herself.)"[63] Contrasting Srey Neth's success to Srey Mom's failure, Kristof suggests that working in a brothel ultimately enslaves Srey Mom to the point where she decides to return to it even when she has the choice not to return. The title of this segment, "Loss of Innocence," is telling in that it suggests both Srey Mom's lost innocence working in a brothel as well as Kristof's own loss of innocence in his realization that there are "few fairy-tale endings."

One silence imposed in Kristof's narrative occurs when he asks Srey Mom, "Do you really want to leave the brothel?" Srey Mom's reply—that she loves herself and does not want her life to be destroyed by what she is doing now—refuses to answer Kristof's question. It is unclear in Srey Mom's response if "what I'm doing now" refers to her work in the brothel, her speaking to Kristof, or any other myriad activities characterizing her now. Kristof never considers this and instead interprets Srey Mom's statement as an affirmative answer to his question. This exchange can be read as an instance where Srey Mom refuses to speak on Kristof's terms, though Kristof's ultimate narration writes the exchange as about his decision to buy Srey Mom's freedom. Here the violence of trafficking exists beyond the descriptions Kristof offers of abuse and "maim[ed] spirits,"[64] but in the ways such violences are narrated and represented. After all, news "is a social resource whose construction limits an analytic understanding of contemporary life" insofar as such stories rely on typifications and indexes of recognizability, and on the (political, economic) structures through which news medias establish themselves as legitimate and professionalized social actors.[65] These stories thus help map representational mechanisms and framing assumptions that dictate both how and at what cost human rights subjectivity is conferred.

4. Seeing Race and Sexuality
Origin Stories and Public Images of Trafficking

THE VISUAL MEANINGS attached to sex trafficking, particularly as they are depicted through official U.S. government sites, reveal the ways trafficking is not only an international issue, but also one that is deeply implicated in meaning making around U.S. national belonging. It is in the visual realm that the stakes of specifying the particular bodies prone to victimization are made explicit. Even though state documents continually point out that "there are no precise statistics on the extent of the problem and all estimates are unreliable," they nonetheless proclaim that "the largest number of victims trafficked internationally are still believed to come from South and Southeast Asia. The former Soviet Union may be the largest new source of trafficking for prostitution and the sex industry."[1] Representing potential victims as hailing from specific places and thus looking a particular way not only threatens to overlook other possible victims, but it also helps reproduce connections between ideals of sexual normalcy/deviancy with national belonging and helps naturalize visual cues with racial categories and cultural communities.

This chapter is anchored in an examination of visual representations accompanying state documents in order to make clear the sexualizing and racializing logic central to producing meanings around human difference and to connect this meaning making to the conferring of humanity and U.S. national belonging anchored in liberal notions of capitalist relations. The chapter opens with a consideration of how the visual imagery of sex trafficking constructs racialized and gendered understandings of national belonging, while the latter sections examine the significance of juxtaposing Eastern Europe and the former Soviet Union with Asia as the two most often noted places of sex trafficking's origin as conveyed in state and NGO documents. Building on the previous chapter, this chapter looks at the specific meanings attached to the cultures constructed as complicit in trafficking.

By examining the "transnational ways of looking" that visual imagery of victims of sex trafficking elicit,[2] the visual logic accompanying (racial, sexual, national, and labor) regimes of human difference are made explicit. These logics distinguish the inner (spiritual/intellectual) self from the outer, physical body presumed to indicate and reflect the inner soul. Such logics are intimately tied to the philosophical and ontological investments of the Enlightenment and post-Enlightenment texts on man, where "the racial writes Europeans and the others of Europe as subjects of exteriority, [which] institutes the body, social configurations, and global regions as signifiers of the mind."[3] Examining the racialized difference of femininities depicted in sex trafficking imagery reveals the ways neocolonial configurations of power—that is, the kind of power relations that enabled colonialism and the consolidation of European Empire during the late eighteenth and nineteenth centuries—continue to inform how human rights works as a site where bodies are sorted and hierarchized.

State documents disproportionately represent trafficking victims as immigrants—nonnationals who are outside the normative parameters of national citizenship. Along with trafficking narratives, visual imagery featuring victims assumed to be nonnationals works to demonstrate the global and national register of race as well as the racialized ways U.S. national belonging is imagined. The national and global registers help to define the concept of racial difference, where racial categories gain meaning through the evocation of a global landscape and national outside. Race as a concept is defined with and against the conceptual register of nation, where differential claims to national belonging work to give individual racial categories meaning. How this plays out in defining the parameters of trafficking victims conceives of human rights as a site where uneven relationships of power can continue rather than a site where such uneven relationships might be addressed.

Racializing Sexualities: Asian (American) Racial Formation

The visual mediums through which antitrafficking campaigns represent victims demonstrates the way such sites work to create and shape meanings around race, sexuality, and national belonging. In the Department of Health and Human Services' (DHHS) "Look Beneath the Surface" antitrafficking campaign (part of the DHHS Administration for Children and Families), a blurred image of a woman in a crowd is accompanied by text that asks readers to

Look beneath the surface: Human trafficking is modern-day slavery. A victim of trafficking may look like many of the people you help everyday. Ask the right questions and look for clues. You are vital because you may be the only outsider with the opportunity to speak with a victim. There are safe housing, health, immigration, food, income, employment, legal and interpretation services available to victims but first they must be found.

Similar to the Immigration and Customs Enforcement's 2009 public service campaign "Hidden in Plain Sight," the DHHS campaign is also directed at vigilant citizens who might "look beneath the surface" to identify human trafficking. The blurry effect of the image suggests the hidden nature of trafficking as an activity that cannot easily be seen without a trained and attentive eye willing to "look for clues." Lacking color, the image represents the starkness and anonymity of trafficking. The only part of the image in focus and clear enough to be distinguished is a woman's face, which appears Asian and is rendered the focal point by being boxed. Posted in public venues—for instance, city buses and billboards—across the United States, the poster is available in English, Spanish, Indonesian, Chinese, Korean, Thai, and Vietnamese.[4] In a city like San Francisco, with a large and historically visible Chinese American population, the DHHS poster campaign does more than appeal to the Asian (immigrant) victim and (American) potential rescuer. It helps produce "Asian Americans . . . born in the United States with formal U.S. citizenship" as "alien citizens" who, despite citizenship, "remain alien in the eyes of the nation."[5]

The fact that "Look Beneath the Surface" is a campaign the DHHS specifically lists as targeting immigrant populations helps to affirm and recirculate the racialization of Asian difference as perpetually foreign, where "the American *citizen* has been defined over against the Asian *immigrant*" and where this difference is apprehensible visually through the body.[6] In part due to the persistent focus on trafficking across (rather than within) national borders, the poster identifies the Asian woman as a likely nonnational victim of trafficking (Figures 1 and 2). In doing so, the image works to further racialize Asian difference through the axis of national belonging, where immigrant status is rendered a more acute part of how some immigrants can identify, and the

Figure 1. Part of the Rescue and Restore campaign launched in 2004 and 2005 by the Department of Health and Human Services, this antitrafficking publicity poster represents a potentially hidden victim of trafficking.

Figure 2. Department of Health and Human Services publicity poster representing a young female Asian victim of sex trafficking as part of the Rescue and Restore campaign launched in 2004 and 2005.

category *immigrant* works on a national scale to connote first and fore-
most Asian and Latino bodies (over bodies identifiable as white, black,
or indigenous). The visible cues conveyed on the body work to mark
the differential claims to national belonging, making racialization always
also about citizenship and national belonging.

The only explicit anti-sex-trafficking (as opposed to human trafficking more generally) poster that is part of the DHHS "Look Beneath
the Surface" campaign also features an image of a young Asian woman's
face. The accompanying caption reads:

Any child engaged in commercial sex is the victim of human trafficking. Children made to work against their will (such as in farm labor, domestic servitude
or sweatshop factories) are victims of human trafficking. There are safe housing, health, immigration, food, income, employment, legal and interpretation
services available to child victims, but first they must be identified.

Curiously, this poster, even while suggesting that children forced into
labor are victims of trafficking, also indicates that employment is one
service the DHHS can offer to child victims. The mixed message works
to draw a line between good (state approved/sanctioned) and bad
(forced) work. According to the poster, commercial sex, whether forced
or not, is always a matter of child trafficking, while farm labor, domestic servitude, and sweatshop work only victimize children when they
are forced into these situations. These images of victims trafficked for
sex work play on notions of gendered infantilization, and they also re-
call and help entrench the racialized sexuality of Asian difference, which
ties Asianness to sexual deviancy and specifically constructs Asian femininity as hypersexual—as "sensuous, promiscuous, but untrustwor-
thy."[7] Thus meanings around racial difference not only work through a
national register, but they also function with and through the register
of sexuality and gender, where understandings of normative sexualities cannot be comprehended without also creating meanings around
whiteness.

Whiteness has historically been defined through the mechanizing
of racial purity ideologies, from eugenics and voluntary motherhood
campaigns to interracial sex and marriage laws. Seeing race as an inheritable matter necessarily makes policing the boundaries of racial
categories a matter of sex because race is literally birthed. Maintaining
the color line thus historically necessitated policing sex and sexuality,

particularly reproduction, to keep the idea of racial categories separate and whiteness pure. Even in the so-called postracial context of the twenty-first century, discussions of identity (as "ethnic heritage") utilize a logic that both conflates ethnicity with race and quantifies race, where one's identity is described as the sum of multiple discrete racial parts (part white, part Latino, part Native American, and so on).

Hence racialization, the process of attributing meaning to racial categories, is inextricably tied up with sexuality and gender. The logic of race as a visual/physical and biologically defined marker of discrete categories (Asian, black, Latino, white) is one that has codified the concept of the one-drop rule, though variably depending on historical, regional, and situational context. For example, with the Virginia Act to Preserve Racial Integrity of 1924, keeping track of blood quantum became a necessary part of ensuring that interracial marriages did not take place and disrupt the racial order. This law helped codify the ordering of society through heteropatriarchal white privilege by ensuring that interracial offspring whose blood quantum was not pure enough ("one-sixteenth or less of the blood of the American Indian and have no other non-Caucasic blood")[8] were never able to claim whiteness. By policing interracial sex and marriage differently depending on how the parties involved could appeal to socially acceptable scripts of behavior, this law also protected white men's access to both white women (almost exclusively) and women of color without the threat of undermining the racial order.[9]

Sexualized racialization is a process that is relational, where the meanings attached to normative understandings of sexuality are relationally constructed against notions of sexual deviancy. The racial register helps to produce some sexualities as deviant over and against others, thus upholding heteropatriarchal ideologies of white purity by justifying constructions of men of color as sexual threats and women of color as sexually available.[10] Racialization is relational also in the ways understandings attached to whiteness, blackness, Asianness, indigenousness, and Latino difference are constructed with and against each other, as well as in relation to the historical, political, and social context.[11] Thus understanding the differential representations of trafficked sexualities demonstrates the ways racialized understandings of sexuality become regulatory norms, where whiteness works to anchor sexualities as normative (evident in the late nineteenth- and early twentieth-century cult of domesticity, for example).

These differential representations of racialized sexualities are apparent in the kinds of images included in a Department of State photo gallery. The Office to Monitor and Combat Trafficking in Persons makes available photographs taken by Kay Chernush to help "illustrate the State Department's annual report on 'Trafficking in Persons.'"[12] The online gallery of photographs titled "Sexual Exploitation" features nine images, seven of which either visually or textually feature Asia (three featuring India and Nepal, the others featuring East or Southeast Asia). Of the other two photographs, the first is an ambiguous image of men standing outside a strip club (with no identifying caption, but taken in Hong Kong according to the file title), and the second is a photo of the back of a woman talking to someone in a car with a caption identifying the site as Western Europe (Figure 3). The caption to the photograph reads,

This woman used in prostitution in Western Europe is forced through threats and intimidation to give all earnings to her trafficker. The amount varies between 200 and 400 Euro ($250–$500 USD) per month. These fees come on top of a huge bogus "debt" typically about $35,000 Euro ($44,000 USD) owed by the woman to the trafficker who brought her, usually from Africa or Eastern Europe. Wealthy European countries are magnets for sex trafficking.[13]

Figure 3. A woman leans into a car in a representation of sexual exploitation.
Photograph by Kay Chernush taken in 2005, courtesy of the U.S. Department of State.

This is the only image in the gallery that explicitly identifies Europe in relation to sex trafficking. The caption situates the image within Europe, and by doing this evokes white victims even though the photo itself is ambiguous, neither revealing the face of the presumed victim or any explicit activity indicating sex. In fact, this is an image that conjures sex only insofar as the image of a woman leaning into a car is overdetermined by shared cultural knowledge of women working the streets and insofar as the caption suggests that the photograph depicts prostitution. The juxtaposition of this image, the only one referencing Europe, with the other images in the gallery demonstrates the relational construction of femininities.

The remaining eight photographs in the gallery either visually or in captions refer to Asia. They are not as ambiguously about sex; nor do they depict women in such modest ways. Figure 4, which follows the Europe image, states in the caption:

Bar girls, like these young women in Southeast Asia, are typically trafficked from impoverished rural communities and neighboring countries. They are required by the bar's owner or "mama-san" to entice male patrons to buy drinks for them. If they do not meet their monthly quota, they may be beaten or brutalized. Other girls work in discos and massage parlors where sex is for sale.

Figure 4. Two women perform on stage while a man looks on. Photograph by Kay Chernush taken in 2005, courtesy of the U.S. Department of State.

The caption implicates all Southeast Asian women in trafficking, whether they are victims or victimizers like the mama-san. In contrast, the image of sex trafficking in Europe represents the activity as an individual transaction between women working the street and potential johns spatially distanced by the car; there is no mama-san, and there is no reference to an organized sex industry (bar girls, massage parlors). Representing sex trafficking through the image of the single woman working the streets (Figure 3) in contrast to an entire organized sector of the economy that passes as legitimate has the impact of making sex trafficking seem like a much more prevalent activity in Asia when compared to Europe.

After this photograph (Figure 4) is one similar to the Europe photo. While the location of the photograph is not specified in any caption, background cues—lanterns, Asian-looking people—and the fact that the previous image describes how "young women in Southeast Asia . . . are required . . . to entice male patrons" suggest that this photograph also depicts a scene in Southeast Asia (Figure 5). The photo file's identifying title, only visible in downloading the image, does in fact indicate

Figure 5. Two women talk to two white men in a representation of sexual exploitation. Photograph by Kay Chernush taken in Thailand in 2005, courtesy of the U.S. Department of State.

that it is taken in Pattaya, a city in Thailand famous for its beach resorts and its relative proximity to Bangkok. This image, which in many ways mirrors the sixth photograph in the gallery, depicts another street scene with two women working the streets, though it is more gratuitous in conveying sex. The image is not ambiguous: men are clearly soliciting illicit activities. It coveys this fact by blurring the men's faces. The two white men are also in direct conversation with the identically barely clad backs of two Asian women, and there is no automobile to distance the parties involved.[14]

The image's referencing of white, as opposed to Asian, johns both makes the transaction being represented seem more elicit in its heralding of interracial sex even while it is also a more palatable elicitness *because* the image involves white men with Asian women (Figure 5). The interracial configuration of Asian women with white men has been made more socially acceptable in the United States as a result of the racializing of Asian femininity as compliant and potentially assimilable while also desirably exotic.[15] As Laura Kang argues, a dense archive of visual representations of the Asian American female makes this figure legible only in some ways and not others, namely as part of interracial and heterosexual relationships with white American male figures. This casting suggests that "the only way to project [the Asian American woman] as *American* is to render each such visible body as genuinely desiring and finally choosing this particular union [with a white male figure] . . . [though] the Americanization of these women is not fully secured but projected with struggle and force."[16] These constructions of Asian femininity with white masculinity have historically helped negotiate race relations domestically, justify U.S. militarism in Asia, and consolidate U.S. political power in international relations, particularly during the cold war and civil rights eras, by representing Asian difference as needing and willing to be domesticated (in contrast to blackness).[17] Further, the visual archive representing Asian female–white male interracial relationships also helps to "encode the 'white male body' as 'American' by way of its emplotted self-realization through interracial, heterosexual desire."[18] Thus by implicating white men, the Department of State image is able to reproduce a sense of American national belonging anchored in whiteness (over and against the foreignness of the Asian bodies). Hence the message of the image can appeal to white and Western audiences by suggesting there is a national and cultural responsibility to address "our" moral lapses when traveling abroad.

The very different ways Asian women are photographed in comparison to their European counterparts suggests that the terms for understanding victims of sexual trafficking diverge depending on the regional and racial identity of the victim, where assumptions about the difference between the female sexuality of the white European victim to that of the Asian woman underwrite the associations the images and accompanying text convey. It is no coincidence that the images used to depict the victim of sexual trafficking hailing from Europe tend to represent the photographed women in a less overtly sexualized manner than those depicting women from Asia. It is also no coincidence that the images of European victims exist alongside those of Asian women.[19]

While these photographs generally do not directly implicate Asian masculinity, rather more often depicting white masculinity, as in Figure 5, it is the implicit assumption that the deviancy of Asian masculinity allows for sex trafficking to continue to exist that underwrites the two contrasting frames for understanding sex trafficking and sexuality. The largely unrepresented but always present implication that Asian patriarchy and (failing) masculinity is at the root of sex trafficking in ways that white Euro-American patriarchies are not forms the crux of the relational construction of racial difference. Further, the juxtaposition of the European to Asian victim also works to racialize Eastern Europe and the former Soviet Union as white and racially homogenous. While the whitening of Eastern Europe and the former Soviet Union has been a process that has taken place within the context of U.S. racial formation since the late 1800s, the particular ways Eastern European ethnic difference is racialized through the site of trafficking demonstrates the particular political context of the post–cold war human rights period where gender and feminism operate as acute axes through which (moral, economic, political) development is assessed.

Racializing Patriarchies, Whitening Eastern Europe

The contrasting of femininities through visual cues offered in state documents is also elaborated in discussions of origins—discussions of why sex trafficking is more likely to occur in Eastern Europe, the former Soviet Union, and Asia than in other places. These explanations racialize patriarchies in a manner that constructs Asia as perpetually bound to patriarchal traditions, while patriarchy in Eastern Europe and the states of the former Soviet Union are constructed in contrast as neither traditional nor despotic. This racializing of patriarchies helps to whiten Eastern Europe and the nations formerly part of the Soviet Union over and against Asia and other regions racialized as nonwhite. The whitening of Eastern European and former Soviet ethnicities echoes theories of civilizational development, where communism in Europe is cast as having kept these regions from progress and the fulfillment of the spirit of capitalism. It also works to represent these regions as racially homogenous, in contrast to the representation of the United States as multicultural.[20]

The difference of patriarchies thus plays a crucial role in framing sex trafficking's narrative of origins, where constructions of Asian difference link Asianness to despotism and traditional practices of patriarchy in ways that gauge progress through the (cultural) exercise of liberal feminist principles. Such representational effects enable human rights to act as a site of (neo)colonial power. The contrastive and relational femininities represented in the state department's image gallery is further reproduced in state and NGO documents, media, and scholarly research explaining why sex trafficking persists in Eastern Europe, the former Soviet Union, and Asia.

Victor Malarek, a journalist, and Andrea Bertone, the director of HumanTrafficking.org, articulate a claim that appears to be taken for granted as part of the story of origin accompanying sex trafficking, namely that trafficking for sexual labor finds very old origins in Asia, while only appearing more recently in Eastern Europe and the former Soviet Union. Malarek states,

The international bazaar for women is nothing new—Asian women have been the basic commodity for years, and armies of men still flock to Bangkok and Manila on sex junkets. Over the past three decades the world has witnessed four distinct waves of trafficking for sexual exploitation. This latest traffic from Eastern and Central Europe has been dubbed "the Fourth Wave," and the speed and proportion are truly staggering. . . . The first wave of trafficked women came from Southeast Asia in the 1970s and was comprised mostly of Thai and Filipino women.[21]

Similarly, Bertone notes,

Prostitution has existed for thousands of years in many different societies. However, South and Southeast Asia are one of the original areas of the world where sexualized work and sex trafficking developed. For example, Thailand's sex tourism can be traced back through local forms of prostitution and concubinage, and colonial sex trading. . . . After Asia, Eastern Europe and the former Soviet Union are extremely fast growing markets for young women. . . . Since the fall of Communism, criminal networks have flourished.[22]

Both Malarek and Bertone suggest that sex trafficking is older in Asia, and in suggesting that the postconflict situation in Eastern Europe and the former Soviet Union has enabled "criminal networks to flourish" and thus traffic women into sex work, the authors criminalize Asian culture, which provides the traditions that enable sex trafficking. The understanding that sex trafficking appears in Eastern Europe and the former Soviet Union only recently as a result of political and economic instability after the collapse of the Soviet Union is contrasted to the explanation that sex trafficking is part of a long-standing historical and cultural practice linked to prostitution, concubinage, and sex tourism in Asia. A key Congressional Research Service report similarly states that "economic dislocations caused by the transition following the collapse of Communism in the former Soviet Union" result in trafficking in Eastern Europe, while practices of "favor[ing] sons and view[ing] girls as an economic burden" explain trafficking's prevalence in the third world, namely Asia.[23] In a 1999 congressional hearing on sex trafficking in Europe, Representative Christopher Smith (R-N.J.), a coauthor of the bill that would pass a year later as the VTVPA, echoes such sentiments, noting,

Although trafficking has been a problem for many years in Asian countries, it was not until the end of communism in East-Central Europe and the break up of the Soviet Union that a sex trade in the OSCE region began to develop. . . . As traffickers know very well, other populations of particularly vulnerable women can be found in conflict and post-conflict settings. [24]

These explanations situate sex trafficking in Asia as "a problem for many years," deeply ingrained in the social and cultural landscape of the region.

The Clinton administration's initial official effort into the research and legislation of trafficking in the late 1990s coincides with the collapse of communism in Eastern Europe and the former Soviet Union. Not surprisingly, trafficking is therefore a central part of U.S. attempts to understand this postsocialist context, where the condition of Eastern Europe and the former Soviet Union after communism is articulated and rationalized through frames of human rights (failures, for the most part). What is telling is the lack of any discussion of trafficking in the region before 1992. In an International Organization for Migration (IOM) study on sex trafficking in the Russian Federation, for example, precollapse Russia is never part of the story.[25] Sex trafficking, explained as a result of regional political and economic instability resulting from the collapse of the Soviet Union, is largely cast as appearing in the region only after this moment, where "material changes in living standards" changed the mind-sets of the "people of Russia."[26] In contrast, another IOM report that examines trafficking in Cambodia identifies cultural precedents as the key reason women are trafficked into sex work and remain in that industry. This IOM report focuses on the "semi-parental relationship" between traffickers and victims that is used to "manipulate women and girls" and emphasizes the role of "cultural norms, such as gender-based norms" in "sustain[ing] trafficking practices."[27] While this may be the case—cultural practices can and do help sustain gender violence—the focus on cultural factors in explaining sex trafficking in certain places and not others, as well as the temporal frames of progress and modernity implied in such explanations, does more than help explain trafficking; it also signals and helps shape racial, national, and gender/sexual discourses.

This framing of sex trafficking in Eastern Europe and the former Soviet Union as a more recent phenomenon assumes that the activity is momentary and will disappear as economic and political stability is restored to the region. In contrast, the problem of sex trafficking in places like South and Southeast Asia is presented as much more deeply rooted—rooted in such a way as to make the practice innate and thus a matter that cannot simply be addressed through good governance. Thus these contrastive explanations of sex trafficking suggest that patriarchal practices are inherent to the peoples and locales of Asia, finding deep historical and cultural roots, and construct Asia's patriarchy as more problematic, demonstrated in the fact that old practices (like concubinage) are finding new outlets. For instance, as Siddharth Kara explains with regard to contemporary sex trafficking activities in Thailand, "the history of Thai women being held as male property dates back to the fifteenth century. As codified in law, men . . . could sell wives as slaves."[28] Unlike Eastern Europe, the existence of sex trafficking in Asia is cast as a matter that extends beyond governance and reaches to a cultural aspect that preexists the state and modern economic relations. This juxtaposition is suggestive for several reasons.

First, the presumed visual apprehension of culture on the bodies of Asian trafficking subjects demonstrates how the language of culture works to racialize postcommunist states through the lens of whiteness in contrast to their Asian counterparts. The whitening of Eastern Europe and the states that formerly comprised the Soviet Union renders invisible people who might look Asian but who identify culturally, nationally, and linguistically with Russia and other states formerly of the Soviet Union. This construction of the former Soviet Union in particular narrowly understands Russia and other former Soviet states as more European than Asian, even though the Soviet Union was predominantly situated on the continent of Asia, an effect that follows cold war epistemologies. As Jodi Kim traces, during the early post–World War II period of the cold war, the Soviet Union was initially understood in U.S. policy documents through an orientalized rationale that racialized it as Asiatic. However, the rise (or fall) of China to a communist regime in the 1950s shifted the lenses through which U.S. policy makers framed the cold war and the communist threat. The displacement of the Soviet Union by China in the imagination of U.S. political doctrines and the Sino–Soviet split of the late 1950s rendered the Soviet Union a European figure within a reconfigured cold war framework that bifurcated the Soviet and Chinese fronts into a largely Euro-American cold war political dispute between the West and the Soviet East figured against an actual (imperial) military war waged against the "red menace" of Asia.[29] Furthering this whitening figuration of Eastern Europe and the former Soviet republic erases the historical and ongoing ways Eastern European and Russian ethnic difference has been constructed against Anglo-Saxon, Nordic, and Germanic notions of whiteness in the United States. The constructed and variable nature of whiteness is thus hidden.

Second, contrasting sex trafficking in Asia with that in postcommunist Europe works to situate racial difference in geographical terms, where Asian difference is perpetually linked to an imagined physical and cultural cohesion defining, namely East (and marginally South) Asia. This logic applies beyond categorically constructing Asian and white/Euro-American difference, and it applies also to the understanding of other racial categories, where, for example, blackness in U.S. racial formations gains meaning through its tie to an imagined cohesive geographical (and cultural) outside (Africa). This operation demonstrates the global complexion of race. Defining racial difference through geographical terms works to help construct the United States as a frontier for race relations and as an exceptional space where such relations might be overcome through the creation of temporal and spatial distance between nonwhite bodies and their racial consciousnesses (the goal of assimilation theories). This racializing work of sex trafficking discourses is the focus of the next chapter. Finally, the contrasting narratives of sex trafficking's origins also reinstill frames of civilizational progress that are racialized and affirm modern regimes of knowledge, where man's distinction is tied to his ability to progress out of a state of nature into the rational realms of jurisprudence and social contracts. The framing of man as developing along linear patterns where more civilized men represent the actualizing of rationality (and capitalism) that less civilized men have yet to grasp constructs global others as "not yet," a construction that enables the upholding of the promise of modernity while naturalizing its teleology.

The ways in which cold war and postsocialist constructions of Eastern Europe and the former Soviet Union situate these regions in between the civilized and modern West and the tradition-bound third world is conveyed in sex trafficking's narration of origins. Samuel Huntington most notably revives the sentiments of Max Weber that the Orient is plagued by despotism, hierarchizing the globe's civilizations into a paradigm where Euro-American or Western society represents the most advanced social organization indicated by the nature of capitalism operating in this region. Asia, by contrast, while advanced beyond African and indigenous regions (where only the possibility of civilization exists, according to Huntington), remains unable to inhabit the civilizational greatness of the so-called West due to its cultural tendencies that pervert capitalism—cultural tendencies that are reproduced through the literal birthing and social rearing of cultural citizens, making this discourse of difference dependent on sex/gender. As Huntington sums up, "Non-Western civilizations have attempted to become

modern without becoming Western. . . . They [non-Western civiliza-
tions] will also attempt to reconcile this modernity with their traditional culture and values."[30] In this schema, Eastern Europe and the
Soviet Union are situated as second world nations momentarily falter-
ing from modernity (as it is captured in the spirit of capitalism) as a
result of adherence to communism. Sex trafficking narratives that often
contrast geographical origins use this notion of a momentary lapse tied
to communism in order to explain the region's failure to ensure human
rights, where in a postsocialist context human rights becomes the gauge
of civilizations.

By now well critiqued for advancing reductionist and racist understandings of (moral and economic) development, the tendency to understand why sex trafficking develops in different regions of the globe,
namely Eastern Europe and Asia, nonetheless reveals the continuing
salience of such troubling lenses to explaining global phenomena.[31]
This racialized lens of civilizational development alluded to in the di-
verging narratives of origin reveals that while the language and terms
do not necessarily name race, the process and effect of creating and
reasserting the innate and natural difference of "other" places like Asia
nonetheless deploy the very logics, assumptions, and operations of racial
power. Thus racializing discourses need not name race to perform the
same work.

On the Path to Modernity:
Universalizing Liberal Feminisms

The naturalizing of liberal principles through the use of teleological
frames of civilizational development not only reassert racialized understandings of modernity and tradition, but also frame the notion of
women's human rights narrowly in terms of achieving the ability for
self-conscious (and rational) choice, where (neo)liberal and rational
capitalist relations are implied as congruent with women's human rights.
The ways in which the racial and national registers help frame sex
trafficking are visually conveyed in a United Nations Office of Drugs
and Crimes–produced public service announcement, "Work Abroad"
(2001).[32] One of a series of several announcements distributed in the
early 2000s, "Work Abroad" features and addresses women who might
potentially find themselves victims of sex trafficking.[33]

The announcement plays on the idea of women going to work abroad and suggests the dangers of illicit sectors of the economy like sex work. The initial scene of the announcement presents a young white woman in everyday clothes looking much like a college student, with accompanying text reading, "Go work abroad." She is next presented in a setting that recalls a dorm room, and as the camera moves into a close-up of her face, viewers see that the woman is crying. Here the text reads, "Housing will be provided." Viewers are then introduced to the announcement's second character, an Asian woman, who watches as a faceless man (conveyed through his hands and a shot of his torso in a suit and tie) tears her passport in two; accompanying text reads, "No work permit required." The following scene depicts the Asian woman's head and bare shoulders as she is lying on her back, while two, large wrinkled, white (presumably male) hands move down her face and out of frame. The accompanying text reads, "You'll meet new, interesting people." In a similar scene that follows, viewers then see a white man looking into a peephole. The camera shifts to follow the gaze of the man to reveal the white female protagonist dancing on stage in only her underwear, with text stating, "Your own comfortable work space." The next scene presents the white woman again in her underwear counting bills in her bedroom; the camera moves from the woman to a close-up of a needle and rubber tube lying on her bed. After this scene, the Asian woman stands in a hallway with a man, who is taking a roll of bills away from her; the text reads, "Excellent salary." In the final scene, viewers are returned to the Asian woman lying on her back with shoulders bare, though the hands that were touching her before are no longer visible. Rather, the camera focuses on her face, which is now cringing to convey discomfort, sadness, and/or pain; accompanying text reads, "Are you interested?"

The fact that the kinds of jobs available to many young women when working abroad—au pairs, domestic and care work—might actually entail the same kind of intimate and affective labor as sex work is left absent in the announcement, even though it alludes to such connections through the title. Rather, the announcement draws a firm line that establishes sex work as devoid of intimacy and care by suggesting that such situations are only entered when women are forced or tricked. Thus the announcement rests on the assertion that "good" work is formalized (through wages and taxes) and therefore also a recognizable hallmark of the public sphere, while work that falls outside these formal structures is framed as dangerous in its potential inversion of this public/private distinction.

The visual narrative of the announcement also references the juxtaposed stories of sex trafficking's origins in the context of Eastern Europe and the former Soviet Union in contrast to Asia. In the announcement, whiteness is signified as congruent with independent, autonomous female agents as opposed to the culturally bound, unaware Asian victim. The white female protagonist is clearly presented in the opening scene as a woman who has chosen to live and work abroad, though that choice may be the result of economic desperation or fraud. The presence of her pimp or trafficker is only ever implied, and it is only in the scene that begins with a close-up of a man looking through a peephole that any single shot in the announcement featuring the white woman places her in a shared shot with any other characters, though never a shared frame. While the white woman is the object of the man's gaze, she is nonetheless separated from him by both wall and camera. This is the only scene where the white female character is suggested to be with a man; all other scenes of her present her autonomously in frame.

Comparing the scenes featuring the white woman with those featuring the Asian character suggests that even though the white woman is also a victim, her closest and worst victimizers are the drugs featured in the scene of her counting money. She is thus represented as having the possibility of exercising agency—of being able to make the decision to quit taking drugs. Yet the announcement presents explicit scenes of the Asian female character being harassed, molested, and threatened by anonymous male characters. Because the announcement also does not gesture to any backstory for the Asian female character—she is only presented as victim, from the scenes of her lying naked on her back to the various scenes of her in the hands of men (pimps taking away money, traffickers tearing up passports)—the announcement suggests that the Asian woman never demonstrates self-determination or choice, even if that choice was a bad one leading her into trafficking. "Work Abroad" implies the opposite is true for the white female character, where the opening scene presents the white character as a normal college-age girl who (innocently or stupidly) decides, according to the accompanying text, to work abroad. The announcement echoes sentiments that in

Russia, "a quarter or half of the sex trafficking victims had jobs or college degrees," as John Miller, the former senior advisor to the Secretary of State on Human Trafficking, states.[34] This is congruent with the explanations of sex trafficking in Asia as tied to cultural adherence to traditional (not modern) patriarchal practices like selling daughters, where women are represented as having no sexual autonomy or opportunity for agency. The racial and national frames work to structure the announcement in a way that perpetuates the racializing of Asian sexuality as deviant, gauges the development of cultural communities in terms of patriarchy, and thus reaffirms the kinds of uneven global relationships that enabled colonialism.

These representations of sex trafficking's origins in Asia and Eastern Europe and the former Soviet Union universalize liberal feminist understandings of gender equity. This liberal framing of women's rights works to ensure that rational capitalist relations provide the exclusive mechanism through which women's rights can be achieved. The question of whether cultural communities can succeed in achieving women's human rights through the apprehension and practice of rational capitalist relations is mediated through questions of the extent to which religion has a hold over those cultural communities. The framing of trafficking thus reaffirms assumptions that in places where "practical rational conduct . . . [has] been obstructed by spiritual obstacles, the development of rational economic conduct has also met serious inner resistance."[35]

The relative modernity of Eastern Europe and the former Soviet Union when compared to Asia is measured through the yardstick of religion and liberal feminist indicators—participation of women in "public" life, the ability of women to be self-conscious and rational decision makers, and women's demonstration of sexual autonomy. In casting two different stories of sex trafficking's regional origins through frames of civilizational development and linear progress toward modernity, trafficking documents construct communism as modern in its formalizing of gender equity in the political, economic, and social realms, while religion (namely, Buddhism, Hinduism, and Islam) is posed as a marker of a tendency toward cultural despotism plaguing Asia.[36] For instance, acknowledging the "progressive" ways communist governments formalized gender equity in the states comprising the former Soviet Union and Eastern bloc, the IOM report on sex trafficking in Russia notes,

"Trafficking in women and girls is caused by the compounding factors of economic collapse and unemployment, the decreasing social status of women in the transition to a market economy."[37]

In contrast, explanations of sex trafficking's origins in Asia never indicate that anything but the low social status of women, tied to religious practices, has been the norm for the region:

The trafficking in women and children for prostitution and sex tourism in Thailand involves the most blatant violations of women's human rights. Yet because this phenomenon is under-girded by cultural and religious attitudes, beliefs, and practices, especially regarding gender roles and relationships, that legitimate its continuation, it has largely evaded the efforts of international human rights law to curb its proliferation. . . . Recognition of women's human rights is made especially difficult in Thailand because Buddhist culture views women as socially embedded in family, kin, and community rather than as self-determining, independent individuals.[38]

These explanations define women's freedom in liberal terms tied to ensuring women as self-determining, independent individuals who participate in the legitimate market economy, where sexual autonomy is defined as anchored in a woman's right to individual expression of sexuality (protected by the state). While the lack of a liberalized market economy was negotiated through communist policies of gender equity in the former Eastern bloc, these policies were destabilized in the period of collapse where, according to the IOM, "the biggest problem with the influx of sexualized glamour [that accompanied the region's turn toward capitalism] was that few were able to differentiate between liberalization and exploitation."[39]

In the case of the former Eastern bloc, the region is understood as historically recognizing women's capacities for self-determination in part because of communism's rejection of religion. The implication to the IOM account suggests that the return of women's rights—the return of women's social status and the protection of their formal status as equal members of society—will naturally result once the transition to economic liberalization has stabilized. In the context of Asia, the ascension of women's social status that accompanies rational capitalist relations, while positive because it will allow women greater movement outside the realm of "family, kin, and community," is ultimately cast as negative because it creates more social pressure on women to help support the family, thus perpetuating the selling of girls by family members.[40] Here the cultural inability to understand liberal notions of female autonomy in the Asian context, in part due to the entrenchment of (non-Christian) religion, is used to explain why economic liberalization has not necessarily ensured women's social status but has rather resulted in the perpetuation of patriarchy and sex work (and trafficking) in Asia. Thus such explanations further affirm understandings of economic, political, and cultural development that naturalizes a linear and singular trajectory of development and modernity, where despite economic liberalization in Asia, the region is cast as not yet capable of exercising (modern) human rights principles.

The implicit assumption driving these explanations argues that the difference of patriarchy—the patriarchal cultural values anchored in religion and tradition specific to Asia—explains why these societies lack comprehension of the proper principles of gender equality and capitalism. Thus the logic follows that catapulting these places into a modern and rational capitalist economy will only further harm women. While providing women in Asia the ability to be "self-determined, independent individuals" is central to combating sex trafficking in the region, the narrative creates a culture of culpability where changing the broader culture is also framed as necessary to fighting human rights violations. However, when taken with the ways these cultural explanations are also racialized, tying traditions to geographies that then make values, beliefs, and mind-sets visible on the body, changing the broader culture becomes a self-defeating exercise. The racial frames distinguishing Asian from white victim in the sex trafficking narrative racialize the Asian victim as in need of reform from outside the so-called cultural community. The visual cues distinguishing Asian victims as Asian convey a kind of visual logic that makes cultural reform impossible insofar as culture is reinscribed through the body.

By considering the visual, representations of sex trafficking reveal how the framing of international human rights issues makes it also about domestic discourses of race, gender, sexuality, and national belonging. In the images of sex trafficking, the apprehension of the transnational cannot take place without reference to national discourses of race and citizenship. Thus even while there is a tendency to see human rights as an international concern distanced from the more domestic concerns of race relations and racism, comprehending one requires referencing the other. Further, the way sex trafficking documents also understand

and explain human rights through liberal feminist frames dismisses other ways of conceptualizing gender/sexual justice. Assuming the universality of concepts like women's human rights and the primacy of the self-determined individual takes away from the promise of human rights by allowing human rights to function as a site reproducing the very relations of power that such projects should seek to dismantle. Thus imagery and narratives of sex trafficking's geographical and cultural origins demonstrate the continued ways modern epistemologies (of capitalist development, economic liberalism, the Protestant work ethic, and so on) frame and restrict how sex trafficking is represented as a human rights violation. Feminist concerns regarding the global resonance of gendered violence thus need to do more than catalog. They need to map and deconstruct the onto-epistemological frames through which we come to know women's human rights issues as such.

5. Refiguring Slavery
Constructing the United States as a Racial Exception

SEX TRAFFICKING often gets talked about in a way that not only conflates it with sex work but also with slavery. Given that the U.S. legal definition of trafficking defines victims as those individuals who lack reasonable choices and/or the ability to consent, the desire to connect contemporary trafficking activities with the imagery and language of transatlantic slavery is not surprising. What work takes place when transatlantic slavery is used to understand contemporary trafficking activities? What kinds of racial discourses become salient by using the imagery of transatlantic slavery to describe trafficking? What is the significance of the fact that a national history (of transatlantic slavery) comes to inform the contemporary international condition of human rights?

This chapter looks at the ways evoking the history of transatlantic slavery to describe contemporary trafficking activities in state, NGO, and media documents enables the writing of U.S. national belonging as a universal aspiration—belonging that all are assumed to desire, and belonging that is imagined as available to all. In the post–9/11 context within which trafficking has become legible as a global and national human rights concern, the framing of trafficking through lenses that historicize U.S. race relations into a progressive narrative works to enable a construction of the United States as an exceptional space of human rights. This construction gauges exceptionalism through the index of feminism and multiculturalism, which allows the state to claim that certain nationalist feminist agendas "overcome U.S. parochialism,"[1] as well as "allow Americans not only to celebrate progress into a more inclusive and tolerant people, but also to tell themselves that this is who they always were."[2] *Multiculturalism* is a term used to describe many racial discourses; here it refers to a way of understanding difference that champions the celebration and inclusion of difference and that assumes the correcting of structural inequalities by civil rights legislations that "equates ending racism with eliminating racial reference within juridical discourse and public policy," thereby imagining a kind of color-blind future.[3]

The ways in which a particular notion of U.S. exceptionalism is forwarded through trafficking discourses demonstrates the limits of inclusion as a political and signifying strategy. While the first half of this chapter maps the methods and effects of equating contemporary trafficking activities to transatlantic slavery, the latter portion considers the limits of discourses of multiculturalism and nationalist feminism that such framings enable. Describing trafficking as a contemporary form of slavery enables a nationalist feminism that "highlights the dangerous thematic and rhetorical linkages between 'progressive' western feminists and conservative nation-builders."[4] These nationalist feminisms work with teleological accounts of racial progress that conflate native-born people of color with immigrants of color; both are written as demonstrating affectable (and thereby needing to be corrected), rather than transparent (universal), consciousnesses—an effect of modern representational strategies.[5]

Framing trafficking through transatlantic slavery helps construct a national project and projection of "the universal force of American norms and institutions," enabling "the belief of U.S. policy makers and public intellectuals that they speak and act on behalf of the entire world," as Nikhil Pal Singh articulates.[6] Sex trafficking works as a site where meanings around U.S. exceptionalism, expressed through a story of racial inclusion and women's liberation, are consolidated through the mythologizing of the history of slavery and its negative effects. The effect of these racial and gender discourses of national belonging is an additive understanding of categories of difference that fails to "move beyond listing how each [race and gender] excludes" subjects.[7] The chapter ends by considering the conceptual groundwork through which sex trafficking narratives reaffirm modern accounts of the conferring of humanity.

Refiguring Slavery

The referential connection made between contemporary human trafficking and the transatlantic slave trade is a rhetorical move that does more than draw attention to the devastating effects of human trafficking. Making these connections evokes and enables a particular way of understanding race and racial discord that writes it into a historical and teleological national narrative. The kind of racial discourse that this reference to transatlantic slavery enables is one that extends the scope of the national to the global. It also frames the U.S. nation as uniquely situated to address trafficking as a global and international human rights issue.

The casting of contemporary human trafficking into the framework of transatlantic slavery is a common rhetorical strategy, evident in media accounts, official state documents, and NGO literatures. For example, one antitrafficking NGO based in Washington, D.C., Polaris Project, names itself in reference to the North Star, which holds significance in slave narratives as the nighttime guide for slaves attempting to escape the South. Indeed, Polaris Project describes fighting "trafficking and slavery in the spirit of a modern-day Underground Railroad."[8] Echoing these rhetorical strategies in a 2004 address to the United Nations General Assembly, President Bush states:

There's another humanitarian crisis spreading, yet hidden from view. Each year, an estimated 800,000 to 900,000 human beings are bought, sold or forced across the world's borders. Among them are hundreds of thousands of teenage girls, and others as young as five, who fall victim to the sex trade. . . . Governments that tolerate this trade are tolerating a form of slavery. . . . We must show new energy in fighting back an old evil. Nearly two centuries after the abolition of the transatlantic slave trade, and more than a century after slavery was officially ended in its last strongholds, the trade in human beings for any purpose must not be allowed to thrive in our time.[9]

This framing of sex trafficking is repeated by myriad other state officials and entities, from the U.S. Department of Health and Human Services to the Department of Defense, the CIA, the Department of Justice, and the U.S. Congress, as well as scholars and researchers like Kevin Bales, president of the NGO Free the Slaves, whose book, *Understanding Global Slavery*, begins with a discussion of the African slave trade in the United States in order to situate contemporary human trafficking.[10] Similarly, former ambassador John Miller, of the Office to Monitor and Combat Human Trafficking, notes, "Most Americans are stunned to find slavery still exists in the United States, let alone the rest of the world. . . . We are beginning to understand the tricks of today's human traffickers, which are the same tactics as those used by the slave masters of old: deception, fraud, coercion, kidnapping, beatings and rape."[11]

Antitrafficking enforcement and litigation is framed through the rubric of civil and property rights, and the VTVPA is understood as an extension and supplement to the Thirteenth Amendment, which further characterizes contemporary trafficking activities as part of a legacy with origins in the transatlantic slave trade and its eventual abolishment. As Senator John Cornyn (R-Tex.) notes in his 2004 opening statement during a hearing before the Subcommittee on the Constitution, Civil Rights and Property Rights:

> As we continue to fight to protect the American way of life in our war against terrorism, we have also been fighting another war to protect American ideals and principles, a war against an old evil—human trafficking and slavery.
>
> Most Americans would probably be shocked to learn that the institutions of slavery and involuntary servitude, institutions that this Nation fought a bloody war to destroy, continue to persist today, not just around the world, but indeed hidden in communities across America.
>
> It has been nearly two centuries since the abolition of the trans-Atlantic slave trade, and well over a century since the ratification of the 13th Amendment. Yet to this day, men, women, and children continue to be trafficked into the United States and coerced into lives of forced labor and sexual slavery. The stories they tell are tragic, disturbing and heart rendering, and the acts that they endure are not just unconstitutional, not just criminal, but profoundly evil.
>
> The experiences that we will hear recounted amount to a modern-day form of slavery. The stories are not easy to hear, but we must hear them and we must face up to them if we are to finish the work of the 13th Amendment and truly expel the institution of slavery from our midst.[12]

Characterizing contemporary human trafficking, and specifically sex trafficking, as manifestations of a "profoundly old evil" performs significant work in several ways.

Framing human trafficking as a new expression of an old evil works to establish a narrative unfolding that, by linking an institution fundamental to the establishment of modern racism to an international human rights issue, casts racism as largely a national problem long past. Transatlantic slavery recalls the institutionalizing of racism, where the codifying of the precept of black inferiority sustained and justified the enslavement of some for the benefit of others.[13] Thus reference to transatlantic slavery also connotes the centuries-old fight to abolish it, which includes the Civil War referenced by Senator Cornyn, as well as civil rights–era activisms aimed at ending institutionalized practices of racism like Jim Crow. This framing thus allows for the assumption that legal revisions like the Thirteenth Amendment and civil rights–era successes like the Civil Rights Act of 1964 have solved the problem of institutionalized racism, which perverted "American ideals and principles" of equality and liberty, leaving the "American way of life" threatened now by contemporary human trafficking.

Yet this desire to situate the institutionalizing of racially based enslavement and inequality in the past ignores the ways structural racism persists and the ways the effects of institutionalized inequality continue long after legal "corrections." For example, as George Lipsitz outlines, despite post–Civil Rights Act legislations to ensure fair and desegregated housing, resistance, refusal, and renegotiation on the part of the privileged did little to alter the status quo, where redlining practices maintained segregated neighborhoods. Additionally, the impact of segregated housing has had lasting effects on wealth accumulation that extend far beyond the passage of the 1968 Fair Housing Act. By the time families of color had legal rights to fair housing practices in the 1970s, white families who had taken advantage of Federal Housing Authority subsidies and tax incentives during the 1940s and 1950s suburban housing boom had accumulated a generation's worth of equity and wealth, demonstrating the continued institutionalizing of the "possessive investment in whiteness."[14]

Further, characterizing contemporary human trafficking as a resurrection of an "old evil," and linking the fight against such evils to an "American way of life," works to write the struggle against slavery and institutionalized racism as part of the national, rather than simply an African American, history—in effect renationalizing black Americans.[15] Bush and Cornyn rewrite and reconcile a divisive and contentious history of slavery, racism, war, and disenfranchisement into part of a shared and smooth national narrative of origin. By casting transatlantic slavery against "American ideals and principles," Cornyn's statement suggests that transatlantic slavery was an aberration—a lapse and error of judgment that, like terrorism, threatened moral principles by introducing evil. Thus characterizing contemporary human trafficking through the lens of transatlantic slavery helps to construct a national mythology centered on the idea of a universally American propensity to fight to uphold equality and liberty—a fight that has enabled a present landscape of racial and cultural pluralism. This national mythology also reconciles the place of U.S. citizens who fought to maintain slavery and segregation by displacing such individuals to the past. In doing so, the fact that slavery and the position of slaves as nonhuman, laboring bodies enabled the institutionalizing of "American ideals and principles" is reconciled.

The fact that the slave was always defined against the national citizen (landowning men) and even against the national ward (wives and daughters of citizens) as a thing never to have claim to the nation and always conceptually outside "American ideals and principles" threatens to pull apart this articulation of the national mythology. In other words, reference to the transatlantic slave trade threatens to expose the fact that slavery was not a momentary lapse but rather a constitutive condition to the founding of the nation-state, providing both a labor force that enabled the accumulation of capital and a conceptual "other" against which the free national citizen could be defined. The retelling of this history through a narrative of sex trafficking that is about "other," non-American lapses of morality works to postpone (by displacing slavery into a contained past) the threat of exposing the very constitutive role of the transatlantic slave trade in the institutional, ideological, and conceptual founding of the U.S. nation. In other words, we might consider transatlantic slavery not as an aberration, but as a constitutive condition. The contradiction of liberty at the core of the U.S. nation is thus reconciled through a historicizing and spatializing narrative of progress that moves outward beyond national borders toward the fulfillment of greater freedoms.

Using the rhetoric and imagery of transatlantic slavery to describe contemporary human trafficking helps to construct the United States as exceptionally situated in global antitrafficking efforts. These characterizations take a historical phenomenon that had a distinctly national impact in shaping the U.S. nation-state and equate it with a global and international humanitarian crisis to appeal to U.S. citizens and, in Bush's case, to the United Nations community. If human trafficking is the new face of the same kind of evils that enabled transatlantic slavery, then those nations and governments that fought to abolish the "old evil" are poised also to lead antitrafficking efforts. Indeed, Bush and Cornyn imply that the historical experience of fighting the evils of slavery place the United States in an exceptional and unique position to lead antitrafficking efforts. This assumption permeates U.S. state antitrafficking discourses, for instance, in the annual Trafficking in Persons reports, which "rank[s] nations according to their status as importers or exporters of trafficking victims" but exempts the United States and also strongly correlates U.S. foreign policy goals with tier placement.[16] In these ways, the United States "has positioned itself as an equally significant [international] force in the anti-trafficking arena" along with the United Nations.[17]

Linking human trafficking to transatlantic slavery makes possible the rewriting of a U.S. history of racial discord and exploitation into a national mythology of progress toward pluralism, equality, and liberty—American principles and ideals—that help legitimate the U.S. role as leader in the global effort to combat trafficking and other women's human rights abuses. Such a move erases the significance of gender and racial violences taking place at home, displacing the impact of "violence, poverty, labor and globalization . . . [on] women of color in our own, local [U.S.] communities."[18] It also upholds a notion of national belonging that is universal (all can now make claim), a universalizing that is furthered through an appeal to a moral law.

Universalizing U.S.-American Principles

Two years after the collapse of the World Trade Center Twin Towers, President George W. Bush, in an address to the United Nations in New York, spoke of the necessity of a global war on terror—a war he described as "between those who seek order, and those who spread chaos; between those who work for peaceful change, and those who adopt the methods of gangsters; between those who honor the rights of man, and those who deliberately take the lives of men and women and children without mercy or shame."[19] Articulating justifications for United States' military interventions in Afghanistan and Iraq, Bush's address shifted to connect U.S. military involvement to the security of a free and democratic globe ensured through United Nations' commitments to arms antiproliferation efforts and other shared work to address "humanitarian crises of our time," including AIDS relief and famine. The other humanitarian crisis that President Bush stressed was the trafficking of women and girls for the global sex trade.

The fact that the President folded the United Nations into the policies and agendas of not only his administration but the U.S. nation as a whole worked to establish a "universalizing force" as characteristic of U.S. institutions and norms. Bush articulated.

> The founding documents of the United Nations and the founding documents of America stand in the same tradition. Both assert that human beings should never be reduced to objects of power or commerce, because their dignity is inherent. Both require—both recognize a moral law that stands above men and nations, which must be defended and enforced by men and nations. And both point the way to peace, the peace that comes when all are free.

By bringing together the founding documents of the United Nations with those of the United States, the president's speech reconstructs the "tradition" underlying these documents as one that is defined by a shared (national and global) effort to extend and include the rights of human beings ensured to them by virtue of a "moral law that stands above men and nations." Noting that the moral law driving both the founding documents of the United Nations and the United States asserts that "human beings should never be reduced to objects of power or commerce," the president refers to the history of the transatlantic slave trade as well as the "modern-day form of slavery" previously noted in the address. As Bush's address describes, sex trafficking is another shared agenda between the United States and the United Nations that is part of a broader global effort to instill peace, order, and moral law even at the risk of waging war.

The national trajectory that Bush projects reads the history of the United States (beginning with the establishment of the founding documents) as one defined by progress toward greater freedom for all, a goal that Bush also casts as defining the United Nations. Thus Bush frames national belonging as a universal condition; the U.S.-American history of greater freedoms is one that is both extended to all and aspired to by all, even those situated outside national borders. This universalizing of U.S. institutions and norms is also ensured by framing institutional responses to global humanitarian crises (including sex trafficking) through the rubric of a "moral law that stands above men and nations." Given the liberal bent of the United Nations Universal Declaration of Human Rights, Bush is not necessarily wrong in suggesting that there is a shared tradition between the United Nations and the United States, especially when it comes to "the idea that the state should respect the human rights of its citizens."[20]

Using the language of moral law and the transatlantic slave trade enables Bush to expand the scope of U.S. laws and legal institutions. Conventional ways of defining human rights do so through the concept of natural or moral law—a law that stands before all mankind— derived from Enlightenment texts on the nature of man and civil society. For example, in defining the origins of political power, John Locke establishes a state of nature—the natural state of man—out of which men reason and decide to enter into social contracts for the mutual protection of life, health, liberty, and possessions. This state of nature is governed by natural law, which, according to Locke, "obliges everyone."[21] The tradition of natural law thus appeals to human rights scholars and advocates precisely because it represents that pristine state before the formation of individual states and governments; it is the universal state of mankind that "all men are naturally in," what for Locke and his legacy is "a state of perfect freedom."[22] Yet this desire to use the tradition of natural or moral law and the state of nature to understand and define the force of human rights limits human rights by privileging the European philosophical traditions of the Enlightenment, out of which the founding documents of the U.S. nation also stem.

Thus the framing of human rights within the scope of moral law helps to ensure the universal potential of U.S. norms, laws, and legal institutions. The national scale of U.S. norms, histories, and institutions is rewritten through a global register, as former first lady Laura Bush's joint 2004 address on the "progress in women's human rights" demonstrates:

Although Abigail Adams, like many women during her time—and since, I might add—handled the domestic duties, she believed that women should have an active role in developing our young nation. . . . Abigail Adams is one of the many women who helped establish the vitality of our nation. Others, like Elizabeth Cady Stanton and Susan B. Anthony, led the determined struggle to gain suffrage for women. And, today, their actions continue to inspire women around the world. . . . The struggle for women's rights is a story of ordinary women doing extraordinary things. And today, the women of Afghanistan are writing a new chapter in their history. . . . We're making progress toward greater rights for women in the Middle East and around the world. But still, too many women face violence and prejudice. Many continue to live in fear, imprisoned in their homes. And in brothels, young girls are held against their will and used as sex slaves.[23]

Under the banner of ensuring the freedom and rights of women in Afghanistan, Mrs. Bush celebrates U.S. militarism abroad and renders a controversial war less so by tying it to a historical and national history of mobilization for the civil and political rights of the disenfranchised (women) that can be applied to the global, and by describing women's human rights violations like sex trafficking as slavery. Her statements demonstrate the salience of what Deborah Cohler describes as a nationalist feminism that appropriates "a liberal feminist language of inclusion by a conservative agenda" that "signals the historical and structural connections between 'liberal feminist' and 'conservative nationalist' discourses of war, peace and nation."[24]

By suggesting that keeping women "imprisoned in their homes" is like holding "young girls . . . against their will and [using them] as sex slaves," Mrs. Bush frames freedom through a liberal and gendered lens that organizes relations through a public/private dichotomy, where greater rights for women globally are tied to the participation of women in the public sphere; hence early suffrage activists Elizabeth Cady Stanton and Susan B. Anthony provide hallmarks for the kind of global feminism that Mrs. Bush proposes. These early suffrage activists were also often active in abolition movements, allowing Mrs. Bush's statement to fold the history of white women's disenfranchisement into a story of transatlantic slavery, the effect of which is to suggest that the United States can lead (because of its national past) global efforts to ensure women's rights.

Yet her version of global feminism conceptualizes politics on assumptions of liberalism, which figure women as equally (and sometimes differently) capable of sharing in a political, cultural, and economic subjectivity that upholds the idea of the rational, self-determined individual. Indeed, liberal feminisms center the notion of abstract individualism at the heart of modern political theories. These notions of abstract individualism "express the essence of the human" at the same time they conceptualize an individual unique from his fellow humans.[25] This contradiction between the abstract and the unique individual is negotiated through difference—where the difference of the individual from the slave, for example, enabled a sense that certain bodies shared in their uniqueness as (human) individuals against their constitutive (slave) "others." Thus "nationalist feminism polices norms of race, gender, and sexuality as it claims to promote neoliberal gender equity."[26] Further, the writing of women's rights into a global frame enables Mrs.

Bush to define women's human rights as a matter for "other" women, which constructs such "others" as behind and not yet capable of expressing the kind of human rights–enacting subjectivity housed in the U.S.-American citizen.

National Mythologies

The universalizing of U.S.-American institutions and norms through the evocation of moral law and the U.S. histories of transatlantic slavery and white women's suffrage helps shape a national mythology that hides and displaces the ways enslavement, exploitation, and disenfranchisement continue to be constitutive in the conceptual and institutional foundation of the U.S. nation-state. Characterizing sex trafficking through the lenses of transatlantic slavery, nationalist and liberal feminisms, and moral law renders the issue of difference and nation only about one conception of the historical struggles for enfranchisement— specifically the struggle for political inclusion narrowly defined as access to citizenship, the vote, and (political, economic, social) representation. These characterizations of sex trafficking thus establish a narrative of progress that is anchored in one way of reading the national history, but that is also framed as universal and global, where the trafficking of women for sexual labor signifies one "last and latest" human rights issue impeding the full actualization of human freedom. As Dr. Laura J. Lederer, director of the Protection Project and senior advisor on Trafficking for the Office for Global Affairs, notes, sex trafficking is "one of the last, unfortunately the last, even in the women's movement the last, of the issues, but definitely not the least, to be examined by our society."[27]

The mythologizing of the history of transatlantic slavery and its rewriting as a national aberration—an evil eventually corrected—rather than a constitutive moment enables a teleological story of inclusion told through multicultural frames that stress pluralism and postracial longings for a color-blind future. In the Bushes' statements, the narrative that frames their remarks imagines the United States as defined by a progressive history moving toward greater freedom and inclusion, a movement that they see as eventually encompassing the globe. Thus the history of the United States that was so fundamentally about extracting the labor of certain bodies without enabling these bodies a claim to the nation, evident both in the history of slavery as well as immigration, is sidestepped. What remains is the consolidation of the history of antiwhite privilege, anticapitalist and antipatriarchal struggles into the mythic discourse of nation that writes the exceptionalism of the U.S.-American condition in the nation's ability to adapt to, include, and celebrate a growing number of racial and national others—an exceptionalism that is (re) told in the stories of Horatio Alger, signified through the Statue of Liberty, and actualized in the election of a black president.

Both espousing and embodying this national mythology, former secretary of state Condoleeza Rice notes during remarks presented at the White House Conference on the Americas in 2007:

> What binds us together is the promise that we carry with us: It is the revolutionary promise that life in the Americas would represent an opportunity for all people—regardless of class or culture, race or religion, blood or birth—to break with the past and begin life anew: to replace poverty with prosperity, injustice with dignity, and oppression with freedom. . . . There was a time, not that long ago, in my lifetime, when whole segments of society were excluded from their rightful place in our democracy—indigenous peoples, immigrants, women, the poor, and of course, in my lifetime, blacks, who, at the time of our founding, were considered 3/5 of a man.
>
> Our history as a nation has taught us humility. It has taught us about our own imperfections. It has taught us never to take our success for granted, and to remember always that our success depends on the broader success of our neighbors in the hemisphere. Most of all, our history, the history of the United States, has strengthened our resolve to be a good, faithful friend to our partners in the Americas—to all work together to build free and better nations, and thereby to inspire others far from our boundaries. . . . Today, as in centuries past, we embody not only the dreams of our citizens, but also the dreams of people across the globe.[28]

Here the "revolutionary promise" of the Americas is rewritten as the ability to offer (capitalism's) opportunities for all people, though this is a promise that was not equally accessible and that continues to need to be ensured. In an inspirational speech, Rice constructs a national sense of belonging and identity as one anchored in a historical and ongoing struggle to "replace poverty with prosperity, injustice with dignity and oppression with freedom" that, when fulfilled, will ultimately include American (hemispheric) neighbors as well as people "across the globe." Rice constructs the promise of the United States as one that moves outward and forward, spatially and temporally, to capture the "dreams of people across the globe" and to move from a national history of disenfranchisement to a global future of freedom. Oppression and injustice are defined through exclusion of blacks, indigenous peoples, immigrants, women, and the poor, thus imagining freedom through multicultural and inclusionary lenses. Rice universalizes the mythology of the United States as a place moving toward greater multicultural freedom by extending it to all of the Americas and the people of the globe. In doing so, she ignores the fact that exclusion was not the principle determining the writing of the racial in all of the Americas, most notably Brazil, for example. Reminding the audience twice that the U.S. history of exclusion was "in my lifetime," Rice also makes her body the evidence of "the nation's transcendence of the racial past."[29] Thus Rice universalizes both the promise of the "American dream" as extending to all people, even those "far from our boundaries," and as including all—blacks, indigenous peoples, immigrants, women, the poor—who symbolize both the nation's exclusionary history and its potential.

The narrative of nation evoked in Rice's speech writes the U.S.-American space through ideals of adaptability, perseverance, independence, and the spirit of discovery, which produces "the trajectory of the U.S. American subject as the realization of the transparent I" or universal subject,[30] where the production of the white body both adhered to and departed from the European consciousness assumed in post-Enlightenment writings of the (global) subject. The (white) American subject was in some ways constructed as the actualization of the Anglo-Saxon European consciousness because its particular American expression rendered it different from its European predecessor in its ability to adapt to the ever-changing landscape of human (racial) differentiation.[31] This exceptionalism of American Anglo-Saxonism tied to the geographical context of the United States is conceptualized against the writing of "Indians, blacks, and Asian immigrants in affectability."[32] That is, these subjects' perceived cultural backwardness offered evidence that such subjects housed consciousnesses (minds, attitudes, and beliefs) needing to be reformed, a fact that was also expressed through these subjects' physicalities. Indians, blacks, and Asians are constructed as "subject to both natural conditions and to others' powers,"[33] an affectability that is in contrast to the assumed transparency and therefore universally desired self-knowing and rational consciousness captured in the white Euro-American body.

This framing and conceptualizing of difference is an effect of modern signifying strategies established through post-Enlightenment regimes of knowledge, which carry through to contemporary writings on race relations, notably in early twentieth-century sociologists' theorizing of immigration and assimilation. These theories worked from the presumption that the melding of races due to the United State's history enabled a unique promise—where overcoming the perceived negative aspects signified through racial difference could be achieved as a result of temporal and spatial distance from one's (nonwhite) racial and cultural origins. One vocal proponent of these theories, Robert Park, father of the Chicago sociologists, "advocated theories of racial difference that focused on the divergent consciousness of groups" where "the physicality of race became secondary to [racial or] cultural consciousness."[34] However, because in some cases the physicality of race would always be in the way of changing the racial consciousness of both whites and nonwhites, Park theorized racial amalgamation as a potential "biological homogenizer," although cultural assimilation—the changing of consciousness—was envisioned as sufficient to end American race relations.[35]

Envisioning race as primarily about cultural consciousness meant racial difference was ultimately a matter of geography, where the difference of Orientals, for example, was an effect of a consciousness bred in the physical space of Asia and thus evident on Asian bodies. Hence Park and other theorists of assimilation saw the distancing of Asians away from Asia (and in proximity to whites) as part of the solution to overcoming racial prejudice, where the different cultural consciousness of Asians might be reformed and allow white citizens to see beyond the Oriental racial mask and recognize more of themselves—recognize that the Oriental is not so different on the inside. Thus, not only do multicultural racial discourses applaud the individual capacity of a woman like Condoleeza Rice to signify a "beyond" race and gender, but they also work to refigure the foreign, nonwhite body into the national mythology as one that can help the nation rewrite its contentious racial history while at the same time universalizing U.S.-American identity.

The assumptions driving Park's assimilation and race relations theories are also continued through multiculturalist and postracial discourses that assume the overcoming of racism through (white) America's conscious choosing to look beyond race. What characterizes these

racial discourses are their ability to advocate a visible move toward pluralism and diversity while simultaneously supplanting the idea of race
(as visible readings of the body) with culture (which references behaviors and practices as distinguishing peoples), where aesthetic markers
come to signify racial difference. The effect of these national mythologies, which frame U.S.-American racial consciousness as moving beyond
race, is a kind of emptying of racial categories so that they no longer
gesture to histories of struggle and inequality, but work only to indicate
a cultural difference among peoples—differences in cuisine, language,
religion, and so on: "To the degree that multiculturalism claims to register the increasing diversity of persons, it precisely obscures the ways
in which that aesthetic representation is not an analogue for the material positions, means, or resources of . . . populations."[36]

Multicultural discourses (re)define racism as either individual acts
of bias that assume a visual logic of reading the body, or as overt institutional calls to exclude on the basis of physical features. By limiting
racism to these instances, multicultural discourses can imagine a postracial future where the "ethno-racial component in identity would loom
less large than it now does . . . and in which affiliation by shared descent
would be more voluntary than prescribed in every context."[37] While
this desire to appreciate the multitudinous expressions of human existence without seeing difference as marked on the body is understandable, the racial discourses linking physical traits to intellectual capacities
cannot be so easily abandoned. Without an understanding of the ways
race continues to operate as a signifying strategy that then helps explain, justify, and situate difference and inequality, multiculturalist discourses simply implicitly reference racial categories while distancing
them from the histories and politics that accompany and help define
them.

Intersecting Narratives, Racial Alibis

The mythology of U.S. multicultural exceptionalism is one that is
enabled with and through narratives of gender and sexual liberation.
The significance of having a black female figure like Condoleeza Rice
espouse the multicultural exceptionalism of American institutions and
history enables a reading of Rice's body as evidence that the nation is
moving beyond its racist and sexist history, where having "black people

stand in for the nation at large" presents a "powerful way to represent the political universality of the U.S. nation-state."[38] Such a move ignores the "unfinished struggle for black civil rights," as Nikhil Pal Singh demonstrates, and displaces patriarchy as a matter concerning other places. Rice both speaks and embodies a particular multicultural national mythology.

The irony and contradiction of "enlisting blacks in the story of the nation's transcendence of the racial past" is that while this move "perpetuates the idea . . . that visible racial difference remains the real deficit and obstacle to be overcome,"[39] this exemplary national subject is at the same time also only captured by the visibly marked body like Rice's that signifies an individual propensity to overcome adversity. Thus these racial discourses work with narratives of progress toward greater gender and sexual liberation, and they privilege neoliberal understandings of citizenship. The visible racial difference to be overcome is often rendered a matter of racial consciousness (bad racial thinking exercised on the individual level that results in Klan memberships, for example); it is not a displacement of the racial knowledges that work to help conceptualize the U.S.-American subject and citizen, nor is it a displacement of the relations of power that figure and necessitate such difference. The fact that multicultural discourses both reject nonwhite subjects as housing affectable consciousnesses and welcome them as symbolizing a future potential demonstrates that "there will always be a tension between difference as benign diversity and difference as conflict, disruption, dissention."[40]

The national mythology of exceptionalism enabled through Rice's speech and sex trafficking discourses reconciles the narrative of American Anglo-Saxonism with a narrative of racial pluralism. Even while the Anglo-American subject continues to signify the transparent and universal national consciousness, writing the U.S. space as housing the capability of affectable consciousnesses to overcome—to potentially reach the kind of universal consciousness signified through the white body—enables the United States also to be imagined as a space of racial pluralism where a black woman like Rice can achieve access into elite political spaces. In immigration terms, this principle drives assimilation theories as well, where immigrants' differential consciousnesses can be reformed to reflect a generic national one, though the success of such reform is already prescribed on the body. Thus the desire to include and assimilate black, brown, and Asian bodies into formal aspects of political and cultural citizenship neither addresses the institutionalizing of inequalities nor alters the ways racial power signifies differential consciousnesses, where the universality of the national subject is written with and through whiteness. Rather, inclusion and representation often end in an empty symbolic gesture, evident in Rice's speech, where physical bodies stand as racial alibis. Thus, even while the work of civil rights–era activisms have been invaluable in addressing inequality in some aspects, the work of addressing racial and gender power continues.

The principle focus on inclusion and representation as political strategies to address racial and gender inequality provides a key limitation to the identity-based politics that have come to shape contemporary national understandings of difference. The logic behind identity-based political activisms enabled disenfranchised subjects to argue a shared experience of exclusion and disenfranchisement. The accounts of the lived experiences of people who identify as disenfranchised on account of their race and gender provide powerful tools in legislating changes to the existing institutional and epistemological structures. Because these political interventions stress, out of necessity, inclusion into existing structures and practices, they articulate their political claims around (equal or just) representation. Thus the visible inclusion of female bodies of color can be read as commensurate with the eroding of racism and sexism in society.

Representational strategies, while important, are limited in the ways the "hailing of 'women of color' [acts] as a synecdoche"[41] for the intellectual and epistemological project of understanding the operations of power that produce categories of difference. How on a conceptual level the notion of (racial, gender) difference enables a particular formation of knowledge—one that finds roots in the Enlightenment and conceives of subjectivity in particular ways, namely, through operations of negation—is connected to, but is not the same as, how the writing of this difference plays out. Representational strategies address how the writing of difference has historically played out; they do not address the onto-epistemological privileging of certain ways of knowing and being: "The domains of political and linguistic 'representation' set out in advance the criterion by which subjects themselves are formed, with the result that representation is extended only to what can be acknowledged as subject."[42] The fact that Rice holds a prominent seat of political power works as a symbolic index indicating the social lessening of both racism and sexism. The representational work of Rice's body demonstrates the limits of inclusion as a sole strategy for addressing uneven relationships of power. It also demonstrates a reliance on an additive understanding of categories of difference that many feminist scholars have long critiqued.[43]

This conflating of bodies—physical ones with bodies of knowledge through which the world is interpreted—not only enables a racial alibi, but also allows for the conflation of immigrants of color with native-born people of color as well as the literal understanding of differences as intersecting on one's body. With regard to the latter, the racial index and gender index are compiled so that a black female body signifies the ultimate position of exclusion as well as the ultimate nonexclusionary position. Under the logic of addition, "woman of color" represents the position of double exclusion (as woman and as person of color) as well as a position of nonexclusion, where she represents the "final frontier—as our temporal and global end" to racism and patriarchy,[44] a logic that posits her inability to enact racism or support patriarchy by virtue of her body. These logics, which see woman of color as the ultimate position of exclusion and the embodiment of a multicultural promise, take the term *intersectional* quite literally.

Such logics enable Condoleeza Rice to perform, simply by being visible, the symbolic function of reassuring a teleological narrative of progress that defines freedom as nonexclusion. The logic enabling readings of Rice's body as a symbolic index of progress also sidesteps the intellectual contributions of self-identified feminists of color who theorized an intersectional approach as an alternative to additive understandings of power. These scholars, working from Kimberle Crenshaw's early work, call for an understanding of the ways the production of categories of difference like race and gender happen simultaneously and in a co-constitutive manner. This understanding of intersectionality works to map how the writing of racial difference depends on certain sexual logics that naturalize particular ideals of gender.[45] As Valerie Smith's work exemplifies, attention to intersectionality is not about "centering . . . black women's experience as such," but about "the practice of reading intersectionally to question the implications of ideological and aesthetic liminality"—a method of analysis and strategy of reading.[46]

The national mythology of pluralistic progress also establishes false analogies between transatlantic slavery and sex trafficking, and between U.S.-born people of color and immigrants of color. The former analogy makes it difficult to consider the activities that fall under trafficking through other lenses. For instance, the analogies established through the use of language like "slavery" and the "American Dream" suggest that the problem of sex trafficking is about individual moral lapses— a lapse for some individuals and cultures that leads to bad human relationships (like that between master and slave) that pervert the principles of humanity. On the other hand, sex trafficking could be considered through a lens that centers labor and capital, which would understand exploitative labor relationships (trafficking activities) and informal economies (like the sex industry) as necessary to ensuring and naturalizing capitalist relations. It is the supposed absence of consent of "victims" and slaves that makes the analogy possible. Yet equating the two activities postpones debates on whether consent should matter in determining whether a situation is trafficking.[47]

In the latter analogy, immigrants of color stand in for the domestic history and politics of race. Immigrants of color certainly become people of color in the United States as they navigate the national racial landscape and their bodies are read into U.S. racial formations. However, assuming an uncomplicated sameness between U.S.-born people of color and immigrants, who in their racialization into the category "people of color" shift and redraw the parameters of the category itself, ignores the long, constitutive history of a national racial struggle—of Asian American, black, Latino, and indigenous people's struggles to make both political and cultural claim to the nation. Failure to consider the different discursive space (one that nonetheless overlaps with that of the U.S.-born person of color) through which the immigrant of color is interpellated also allows for a flattened notion of immigration, one that erases the circumstances prescribing immigrants' arrival and entry like access to wealth, and one that fails to comprehend the global register of racism where dark African immigrants racialized as black in the United States might disidentify from black Americans out of a desire not to be conflated or identified with the stereotypes circulating around African *Americanness*. As Chandra Mohanty and Jacqui Alexander note, women are "not born women of color, but become women of color here [in the United States]."[48]

What Alexander and Mohanty refer to—the way racial formation in the United States reads a black body as African American regardless of whether that body actually identifies with the term—is a process that at once signals the specific national terms of U.S. racial formation even as it exposes the global axis through which national understandings of racial categories are understood. U.S. racial categories have defined themselves in part through an extranational imaginary, one that links being black in the United States to the continent of Africa (hence African American) or that understands being Asian American through the concept of an Asia that is outside the U.S. nation. Here is what is at stake: as a native of Somalia and a Dutch citizen, best-selling author Ayaan Hirsi Ali's body signals "woman of color" in the United States (where she spent time as a fellow at the conservative think tank the American Enterprise Institute). Yet this category is one with a particular national racial formation behind it, one that recalls the work of people like Gloria Anzaldua, Angela Davis, bell hooks, and Cheri Moraga. It is also a category that connotes a kind of political consciousness about the ways race and gender work together to produce meanings tied to U.S. identities. Hirsi Ali's body signals this history of woman of color even while she herself might espouse political goals that are in direct opposition, thus jeopardizing the political and intellectual goals that are about understanding the history of exploitation based on differential understandings of the human body. While Hirsi Ali might not identify as a woman of color, the circulation of her body and text within the United States nonetheless reads her into the history of national racial formation and struggle, making U.S. political and racial formation a part of her personal life whether she sees it as such or not. If second-wave feminists organized under the banner "the personal is political," women of color feminists demonstrate how the political becomes personal.

The danger of not seeing the different symbolic function and signifying work that a nonnational body like Hirsi Ali's performs in contrast to one like Condoleeza Rice, whose blackness is not distanced from the national history of slavery in the same way as Hirsi Ali, rests in the ways multicultural discourses import foreign signifiers of difference in order to empty racial categories of the national context of history and politics while using these signifiers in the rewriting of a national racial history. The importing of foreign signifiers of difference enables the inclusion of racial/cultural difference that, because of their distance from the national history of racial inequality and unrest, poses less threat in exposing such histories. The significance of trafficking discourses to these national mythologies is that its characterization as an activity that victimizes mostly nationally "other" women means that trafficking offers a place where multicultural mythologies of national exceptionalism can be fulfilled. Characterizing sex trafficking as "one of the last, unfortunately the last, even in the women's movement the last, of the issues, but definitely not the least, to be examined by our society" situates women's human rights into a teleological narrative where "saving" nonnational victims also enables the fulfilling of multicultural national narratives.[49] Nonnational victims who are saved and can become U.S. citizens come to symbolize both the mythology of U.S. success as a global human rights leader as well as the related U.S. success as a multicultural and pluralistic society.

Sex trafficking thus acts as a site where the black body is renationalized, and this renationalizing takes place through the insistent signifying of the nonnational female body of color as the last and latest disenfranchised subject waiting to be included in the global dialogue. It is the rewriting of the role of blackness to the nation—a rewriting that enables the (tokenistic) gestures that allow a black woman, a former secretary of state, to speak of things getting better—that resignifies American blackness in a way that deploys racial power. The form and configuration of racial power enabled through the consolidation of global feminist claims and civil rights agendas into the state are not the same as the kind of expression of racial power that reigned during the period of slavery or even after. Racial discourses shift and racial meanings change. What remains constant is the deployment of racial power— racial power that privileges certain forms of knowing and being, namely, those (modern) regimes that centered and universalized the white, Euro-American body as that which captures proper (national) subjectivity.

These national mythologies racialize whiteness as owning the progressive spirit that makes a better future without racism, sexism, or xenophobia possible. The white American body is rendered the progressive agent through which exceptional and universal U.S.-American ideals can be ensured even while they are actualized through the nonnational, racially "othered" female bodies being saved. Perhaps this is most evident in the refiguring of whiteness that accompanies outside efforts to rescue, evident in the story of *New York Times* columnist Nicholas Kristof, who writes about buying the freedom of two Cambodian teenagers he meets in local brothels, Srey Mom and Srey Neth, discussed in chapter 3. Taken into consideration with his general references to slavery, Kristof's decision to buy the girls' freedom cannot but connote a history of white liberal desire, also evident in the mission of the NGO Free the Slaves, which allows individuals to "give the gift of freedom" through online donations.[50] Kristof notes that "readers started sending me frantic e-mails along the lines of: I'll wire you some money if you'll free one for me, too."[51] Recalling both the troubled abolitionist desires like those captured in Harriet Beecher Stowe's *Uncle Tom's Cabin* and also the missionizing impulse of late nineteenth-century feminists like Jane Addams of Hull House fame, the story of sex trafficking and its rewriting of slavery is part of this legacy. Ironically, the buying of freedom only recommodifies those being bought while ignoring questions into the uneven distribution of labor markets, wealth, and power.

The impulse to buy the freedom of a sex slave is in part an effect of the rhetorical framing of contemporary human trafficking through the imagery of the transatlantic slave trade and proliferates beyond Kristof's personal desire to a wide range of organizations, including Emancipation Network, which lists hosting "Shop for Freedom" parties as one way to help combat trafficking.[52] Emancipation Network works to "improve the lives of slavery survivors" by offering education and jobs, where support for the organization comes in part from the selling of "unique fair trade jewelry, bags, and gifts" designed and created by survivors.[53] While it is possible that the survivors whom Emancipation Network aids do find their conditions bettered through the work of the organization, the organization nonetheless also participates in the uneven circuits of capital and labor that sustain the drastic global wealth gap. An organization founded by American Sarah Symons and her husband (a former investment banker), the organization's beginnings are described by Symons this way:

During a tour of the shelter [established by an antitrafficking organization in Nepal], we came upon a small room piled high with sparkly purses and beaded jewelry which were being made as part of the informal education program. Well, it was obvious what to do! I brought a few hundred dollars of samples home and showed them to all my friends and family. My husband John came up with the idea of selling the products at home parties, because this would also allow us to raise awareness about human trafficking.[54]

Forwarding a sense of global sisterhood (Symons has been featured in women's magazines like *Redbook,* and the organization was linked to the Lifetime Television human trafficking miniseries running in 2005 and featuring actress Mira Sorvino),[55] these efforts, despite the individuals they may help, nonetheless reaffirm troubling constructions of whiteness tied to first world economic privilege. Here women's human rights works as a site through which national mythologies of U.S.-American exceptionalism configure and naturalize neoliberal practices as that which enables human rights enactment.

The desire to buy freedom for slaves helps write a national mythology that inscribes freedom through neoliberal principles and universalizes this definition of freedom. The fact that Kristof is a son of an Eastern European immigrant, and the fact that black, Asian, and Latino Americans can also participate in the purchasing of freedom for a sex slave, simply reaffirms a story that reads: "Once only whites, now all Americans." This story further inscribes the United States as an exceptional space where the past (institutional) lapses of morality are presumably corrected to ensure that even those whose difference is marked on their bodies can nonetheless access the kind of transparent subjectivity and citizenship captured in the white Euro-American body. Thus the fact that Latina/os, blacks, and Asian Americans are able to rescue the nonnational Latina/o, black, and Asian trafficked subject demonstrates the exceptional ability of the U.S. space to distance the nonwhite subject from the negative aspects of their cultural difference—a difference that with enough temporal and spatial distance can begin to be corrected (though never fully). Thus these multicultural discourses are not necessarily better but only different in the ways they help shape understandings of race, and their difference lies mainly in the universalizing aspect that helps write national understandings of race through a global landscape of human rights.

Shifting Paradigms

Even while the election of Barack Obama as president in 2008 enabled further framings of difference and national identity through paradigms of progress and even postracialism, the change in political regime has also resulted in small but substantial shifts in how the Department of State discusses trafficking. These seemingly slight but significant shifts demonstrate the power of how changing paradigms impact the day-to-day realities of trafficked subjects—of how changing the conceptual and discursive terms alter the material and real.

One of the most notable shifts in language and frameworks instituted under Secretary of State Hillary Clinton and head of the Office to Monitor and Combat Trafficking Luis CdeBaca is the explicit denunciation of the practice of those with more means of buying "freedom" for trafficking subjects. Pointing out the harmful impact of buying freedom, the 2009 Trafficking in Persons Report notes:

> Among the repugnant aspects of human trafficking is the commodification of human lives: the assignment of a monetary value to the life of a woman, man, or child. . . .
>
> Anti-slavery organizations and activists have sometimes opted to pay the price of victims' freedom from their exploiters. . . . While this releases victims from the bonds of modern-day slavery, the implications of this practice are more complicated.
>
> If trafficking victims are freed because of a payment or negotiation, the trafficker remains unpunished and unrepentant and is free to find new victims to perform the same service. By "purchasing" a victim's freedom, well-intentioned individuals or organizations may inadvertently provide traffickers with financial incentive to find new victims. While the numbers of victims rescued from compensated or negotiated releases can seem impressive, it is difficult to determine whether they lead to a net reduction in the number of victims.[56]

Much of the visual and rhetorical framing of trafficking in the 2009 report remains consistent with previous reports, including seeing trafficking as "modern-day slavery." Yet the addition of a small special-topics section titled "Negotiating or Buying a Victim's Freedom" shifts anti-trafficking efforts away from reaffirming neoliberal practices of consumer activism by pointing out that the practice of buying freedom commodifies human life in much the same manner as trafficking. Here the report moves out of a simple rescuers–victims–criminals paradigm by suggesting potential overlap between rescuers and criminals, enabling a more complicated understanding of trafficking as tied to uneven distributions of global capital.

Additionally, attention to the vulnerability of stateless persons helps the report refocus trafficking on broader issues tied to citizenship and rights. Pointing out the ways refugees and, by extension, all undocumented peoples (specifically named in the report are mail-order brides) are particularly vulnerable to exploitation because they have no legal documentation or status for recourse and protection, the report begins to blur the distinction between trafficking victims and illegal aliens. This slight shift that discusses trafficking in relation to undocumented status can have a real effect on changing the paradigms through which not only trafficking but also undocumented immigration might be re-assessed. The blurring of trafficking victim with illegal alien opens up the possibility of considering labor standards and protections that are not contingent on legal immigration or citizenship status. These are simply two examples of the ways shifting paradigms can open up possibilities for material change.

Understanding how trafficking is framed—for instance, through the language of transatlantic slavery—and what such framings can tell us about our investments and understandings of national belonging, gender and sexual norms and racial difference is just as important a project as documenting exactly what trafficking is. In fact, the project of defining and documenting trafficking is an effect of, and helps shape, the conceptual categories and tools through which we imagine national belonging and human rights subjectivity. The fact that sex trafficking discourse enables a construction of U.S. citizenship as (always) universally attainable demonstrates the ways the conceptual tools and mechanisms for understanding human rights subjectivity are informed by modern signification strategies and post-Enlightenment principles. Thus shifting the terms of human rights necessitates understanding and mapping this conceptual terrain to open up alternative possibilities.

Conclusion:
Considering the Transnational in Feminist Actions

WHEN I HAVE presented various aspects of this work at conferences and as lectures, the question I always receive, regardless of whether the audience is mainly students, academic faculty, or advocates, is, "So what can we do?" The project of cultural critique and conceptual mapping is one that is often seen as distanced from the day-to-day realities of life and the concerns categorically labeled as activist. Thus while audiences have generally been receptive to the critiques of existing frameworks offered in this work, there has also been a perceived disconnect between the conceptual arguments and "real" action. What I have tried to emphasize in this book, therefore, are the very real ways conceptual frames delimit how and what gets identified as trafficking, and who is able to become legible as trafficking subject, whether victim, criminal trafficker, or rescuer. In other words, the concepts shape and help constitute what we come to know and understand as the "real." Focusing on the conceptual side of human rights is a decision I made precisely because I care deeply about the so-called activist question, "So what can we do?"

The answers to this question will remain stuck replaying the same conundrums of reinstituting and taking for granted colonial hierarchies and racist ideologies without an effort to question the very premises of universality assumed in the conceptualizing of human rights. Thus strategies formulated to remedy human rights' neocolonial impulse must contend with the conceptual parameters in order to open up possibilities for using human rights as a tool for betterment. Part of what we do next necessarily entails looking beyond stated and documented facts to seeing the processes, assumptions, and frameworks at work in rendering facts. For instance, it is a fact that victims of sex trafficking sometimes hail from the states formerly comprising the Soviet Union and Eastern bloc. This fact is explained through (and thus helps entrench) racialized and sexualized frames, as well as (neo)liberal assumptions that define gender freedom through participation in politics and legitimated capitalist enterprises, the exercise of choice and female bodily autonomy. Not seeing the processes through which the facts of Eastern European sex trafficking naturalize particular frames and assumptions leaves human rights critiques reasserting problematic hierarchies. Yet it is only because there is already a well-researched body of sociological literature dedicated to documenting human trafficking that this book has the luxury of deconstructing the "truths" of trafficking.

Mapping the dominant discursive parameters through which sex trafficking is produced is only one aspect of the work that needs to take place to alter the existing paradigms through which human rights come to be defined. The other kinds of work necessary to changing existing paradigms include efforts that are often described as grassroots, where those who get written as subjects in need of human rights challenge, question, and redefine the very act of being written as "not yet" or "in need." For example, the women of Sangtin in Uttar Pradesh, India, chronicle the debates and discussions that took place among the seven members, which ultimately enabled them to build an "analysis and critique of societal structures and processes, ranging from the very personal to the global."[1] As their work demonstrates, through sharing, discussing, and exploring the issues that concerned them, they produced a compelling critique of the institutional and discursive structures that the women navigate. They are neither romantic nor cynical about their positions within the hierarchies of NGOs and human rights regimes. Further, the writers never assume that their speech is transparent; they resist a reading of their work as an authentic voice and instead question the desire to authorize their voices, whether for their own personal goals or for the broader goals of the NGO.

The work of mapping the discursive landscape and the regimes of knowledge through which a human rights issue like sex trafficking becomes real to U.S. audiences entails a kind of transnational feminist methodology—a methodology that is attentive to the ways privilege is consolidated through multiple axes (race, gender, sexuality, nation, and so on) unevenly and differentially across and within communities. It is a methodology that is transnational in its attention to the various ways national power, privilege, and identity are consolidated, and it is feminist in its insistence on understanding the relational workings of patriarchal and racial power in shaping social relations. In their seminal discussion of the stakes of transnational feminist practices and methodologies in an era of "scattered hegemonies," Inderpal Grewal and Caren Kaplan call for feminist political practices that seek to recognize the utility of linkages offered through the shared and overlapping notions of woman while also remaining deeply suspicious of any universal impulse. They call for a feminist methodology that "seek[s] creative ways to move beyond constructed oppositions without ignoring the histories that have informed these conflicts or the valid concerns about power relations that have represented or structured the conflicts up to this point."[2] In this way, feminist political practices can utilize the benefits that come out of a (universalizing) category like *woman* while also interrogating how such a category has been constituted. The approach to trafficking and human rights that this book takes is thus one that is interested in understanding and unpacking the multiple ways in which power works to establish truths about trafficking, notably the ways constructed oppositions, which are an effect of modern regimes of knowledge, frame descriptions of trafficking and trafficking subjects in mainstream state, media, and NGO representations. What I hope the book offers to transnational feminist methodologies is a way to also consider race as an analytical category that is central to any discussion of the transnational.

Deconstructing the work of discursive scripts—the taken-for-granted narratives that get attached to certain forms of violence and help shape how such violence is understood—is an important exercise because these scripts impact the ways those seeking state and nonstate protections can navigate available avenues for redress (like the T visa). Asylum is another example where human rights frameworks are mechanized to provide (one of few) avenues for individuals seeking state protection from persecution and violence. Yet as Jacqueline Bhabha, Shefali Desai, Michelle McKinley, Miriam Ticktin, and many others argue, asylum is about much more than providing an avenue for protection. The politics of asylum demonstrate how a conceptual "conflict between two founding principles of modern society—the belief in universal human rights . . . and the sovereignty of nation-states" shapes social realities and establishes limits to what the law can do for human rights.[3] These conflicting principles are negotiated through the mythologizing of the law as both a universal force and a cultural institution—a mythology taken for granted in human rights projects that adhere without question to a principle of universalism.

Thus to move away from the conundrums of human rights—for instance, of providing a site where imperialism and colonialism can be reaffirmed rather than addressed—requires engaging with the concept of universalism rather than assuming it as a discoverable object. What makes the concept of human rights such a powerful and imaginative one is its (modern) capability to capture both a universal force and culturally particular meanings. As Sally Merry's anthropological work examining the vernacular practices of human rights demonstrates, human rights captures not only the conventional definitions validated through state and juridical channels, but also the localized actions reinterpreting and shaping conventional definitions.[4] The conceptual conditions tied to universality, which define it through and against difference, are important to understand because they ultimately constrict how human rights can be used as a political tool even as these conditions also provide the reason why human rights offers almost limitless possibilities for imagining alternatives.

As a human rights violation, human trafficking activities inflict violence on thousands, and while many of the individuals who identify as trafficked find their experiences validated and reflected in the narratives and stories offered by the state, media, and NGOs, others do not. This book considers how certain experiences and narratives gain currency and validity as representing trafficking. It also traces the tropes that serve as narrative indexes of trafficking, and the assumptions behind validated narratives. Considering how a particular profile and narrative gets attached to the terms of trafficking can illuminate what is left unaccounted for in dominant representations. While these dominant victim narratives can and do help individuals seeking to identify as trafficked subjects, they also define what and who falls inside or outside the parameters of such subjectivity. Thus looking at how trafficking and its subjects are described (what assumptions and frameworks are used to sustain such descriptions) is important to recognize those who fall outside existing categories of victimization and to understand how race, gender, sexuality, and nation shape human rights subjectivities and inform contemporary human rights discourse.

Stories and testimonies offered in the courtroom are shaped by and help shape news media accounts as well as state and NGO research.

These multiple sites write trafficking scripts one way and not another, producing discursive conditions through which trafficking subjectivity is conferred. These discursive conditions reaffirm the hierarchized separation of human rights–enacting subjects, human rights–deserving subjects, and criminals. This triad configuration of human rights subjectivity is limiting in its disabling of overlap between and among categories, in essence erasing the ways human rights–deserving subjects might also be criminalized (in the case of undocumented migrants who might also be trafficking victims) and/or enacting human rights (in the case of victims who are not saved by a rescuer but rather find their own ways of altering their conditions). Similarly, there is neglect in considering the ways human rights–enacting subjects are also complicit in human rights violations. Further, the schematizing of human rights subjectivities and the processes through which certain scripts gain legal and cultural currency demonstrate the racial, gender, and sexual discourses salient to national framings of both U.S. citizenship and human rights subjectivity.

Thus sex trafficking offers a unique site where the conceptual conditions of human rights can be explored. As a human rights issue made real within the context of postsocialist and post-9/11 conditions, the way sex trafficking narratives frame and articulate race, gender, sexuality, and poverty demonstrate the salience of multicultural, neoliberal, and global feminist discourses for understanding the contours of both national and global citizenship. Furthermore, the articulation of trafficking through victimization and agency, culture and morality, and transatlantic slavery brings to light the paradoxes and contradictions that set the conceptual terms of the debate—terms that make rights claims always conditional and envision human rights subjectivity through teleological and dialectical relationships.

To the question "So what do we do?" I hope the book presents a compelling reason to consider the representational critique as not disconnected from so-called material action. Mapping the discursive mechanisms that delineate human rights issues like trafficking makes possible the opportunity to see what might otherwise be missed. Throughout, the book has provided alternative readings and questions that are hidden in the naturalizing of particular modes of subjectivity and narratives when describing trafficking. The fact that there are many alternative readings and no clear conclusions is indicative of the complex and contradictory operations of power at work in establishing a human rights epistemology. I was hesitant to write a conclusion to the book in part because there are no conclusions or easy answers, only different and more attentive ways of seeing. It is here, however, that I locate possibilities for change and social justice.

Notes

Preface

1. Sangtin Writers and Richa Nagar, *Playing with Fire* (Minneapolis: University of Minnesota Press, 2006), xxi.

2. Ibid., 146.

3. Inderpal Grewal, *Transnational America* (Durham: Duke University Press, 2005), 129.

4. *University of California Regents v. Bakke* (No. 76-811, 438 U.S. 265, filed 23 June 1978). Available at http://caselaw.lp.findlaw.com/scripts/getcase.pl?navby=CASE&court=U.S.&vol=438&page=265 (accessed July 10, 2010).

5. M. Jacqui Alexander and Chandra Mohanty, "Genealogies, Legacies, Movements," in *Feminism and "Race,"* ed. Kum-Kum Bhavnani (New York: Oxford University Press, 2001), 499.

Introduction

1. Sally Engle Merry, *Gender Violence: A Cultural Perspective* (West Sussex, UK: Wiley-Blackwell, 2009), 28.

2. Saidiya Hartman, *Scenes of Subjection: Terror, Slavery and Self-Making in Nineteenth-Century America* (New York: Oxford University Press, 1997), 5.

3. These estimates are according to the United States Department of State (DOS), the main federal agency coordinating antitrafficking efforts in the United States. The estimates come from the 2000 TVPA.

4. HR 3244, Section 103.

5. In the Senate, Christopher Bond (R-Mo.), Charles Hagel (R-Neb.), George Voinovich (R-Ohio), Fred Thompson (R-Tenn.), and Russell Feingold (D-Wis.) voted against HR 3244. In the House, only Marshall Sanford (R-S.C.) voted against the bill.

6. HR 3244, Section 102b.

7. HR 3244, Section 103.8.

8. HR 3244, Section 103.2.

9. Francis Miko, *Trafficking in Persons: The U.S. and International Response (RL30545)* (Washington, D.C.: Congressional Research Service, January 19, 2006).

10. Vidyamali Samarasinghe, *Female Sex Trafficking in Asia* (New York: Routledge, 2008), 15–17.

11. These figures are according to the Government Accountability Office 2006 Assessment of U.S. efforts to combat human trafficking. *Human Trafficking: Better Data, Strategy, and Reporting Needed to Enhance U.S. Antitrafficking Efforts Abroad,* Report to the Chairman, Committee on the Judiciary, and the Chairman, Committee on International Relations, House of Representatives, July 2006 (GAO-06-825), 1.

12. John Miller, "A Statement on Human Trafficking–Related Language," Washington, D.C., December 15, 2006. Available at http://2001-2009.state.gov/g/tip/rls/rm/78383.htm (accessed February 13, 2011).

13. Rachel Paulose (presentation, Human Trafficking in Minnesota Conference, Neighborhood House, St. Paul, Minn., Friday, September 28, 2007). The conference was hosted by several nonprofit advocacy groups from Minneapolis and St. Paul. The main organizer was the St. Paul legal advocacy organization, Civil Society, where Linda Miller is executive director.

14. Laura Kang, *Compositional Subjects: Enfiguring Asian American Women* (Durham: Duke University Press, 2002), 3.

15. Inderpal Grewal, *Transnational America* (Durham: Duke University Press, 2005).

16. Charvet and Elisa Kaczynska-Nay, *The Liberal Project and Human Rights: The Theory and Practice of a New World Order* (New York: Cambridge University Press, 2008).

17. Iris Marion Young, *Justice and the Politics of Difference* (Princeton: Princeton University Press, 1990).

18. Rachel Lee, "Notes from the (Non)Field: Teaching and Theorizing 'Women of Color,'" *Meridians* 1, no. 1 (2000): 85–109.

19. Alexander and Mohanty, eds., *Feminist Genealogies, Colonial Legacies, Democratic Futures* (New York: Routledge, 1997), xvii.

20. Radhika Coomaraswamy, "Are Women's Rights Universal? Re-Engaging the Local," *Meridians* 4, no. 1 (2002): 16.

21. Lee, "Notes from the (Non)Field," 91.

1. Universalism and the Conceptual Limits to Human Rights

1. For example, Neda Atanasoski, "Roma Rights on the World Wide Web: The Role of Internet Technologies in Shaping Minority and Human Rights Discourses in Post-Socialist Central and Eastern Europe," *European Journal of Cultural Studies* 12, no. 2 (May 2009): 205–18.

2. For example, Michelle McKinley, "Cultural Culprits," *Berkeley Journal of Gender, Law and Justice* 24, no. 2 (2009): 91–165; Sally Engle Merry, *Gender Violence* (West Sussex: Wiley-Blackwell, 2009), 134–55.

3. For example, Haleh Afshar, "Women and the Politics of Fundamentalism in Iran," in *Feminism and Race,* ed. Kum-Kum Bhavnani (Oxford: Oxford University Press, 2001), 348–65; Lama Abu-Odeh, "Post-Colonial Feminism and the Veil: Considering the Differences," *New England Law Review* 26 (Summer 1992): 1527–42.

4. "The Universal Declaration of Human Rights: A Living Document," http://www.un.org/events/humanrights/2007/udhr.shtml (accessed February 13, 2011).

5. American Anthropological Association, "Statement on Human Rights," *American Anthropologist* 49, no. 4 (1947): 539–43.

6. "The Universal Declaration of Human Rights: A Living Document," http://www.un.org/events/humanrights/2007/udhr.shtml (accessed May 16, 2008).

7. Jack Donnelly, *Universal Human Rights in Theory and Practice* (Ithaca: Cornell University Press, 2003).

8. "The Universal Declaration of Human Rights: A Living Document" (accessed May 16, 2008).

9. Beth Simmons, *Mobilizing for Human Rights: International Law in Domestic Politics* (Cambridge: Cambridge University Press, 2009), 42.

10. Clifford Bob, "Fighting for New Rights," in *The International Struggle for New Human Rights,* ed. Clifford Bob (Philadelphia: University of Pennsylvania Press, 2009), 8.

11. Peter Fitzpatrick, *Mythology of Modern Law* (London: Routledge, 1992), 9.

12. Bruno Latour, *We Have Never Been Modern,* trans. Catherine Porter (Cambridge: Harvard University Press, 1993), 28–29.

13. Judith Butler et al., *Contingency, Hegemony, Universality: Contemporary Dialogues on the Left* (New York: Verso, 2000), 35.

14. Susan Okin, "Feminism, Women's Human Rights, and Cultural Difference," *Hypatia* 13, no. 2 (Spring 1998): 35.

15. Hilary Charlesworth, "What Are 'Women's International Human Rights'?" in *The Human Rights of Women: National and International Perspectives,* ed. Rebecca Cook (Philadelphia: University of Pennsylvania Press, 1994), 76.

16. Deborah Mindry, "Nongovernmental Organizations, 'Grassroots,' and the Politics of Virtue," *Signs* 26, no. 4 (2001): 1193.

17. Inderpal Grewal, *Transnational America: Feminisms, Diasporas, Neoliberalism* (Durham: Duke University Press, 2005), 152.

18. Vasuki Nesiah, "Toward a Feminist Internationality," in *Global Critical Race Feminism,* ed. Adrien Wing (New York: New York University Press, 2000), 44.

19. Shefali Desai, "Hearing Afghan Women's Voices: Feminist Theory's Reconceptualization of Women's Human Rights," *Arizona Journal of International and Comparative Law* 16 (1999): 833.

20. Uma Narayan, "Essence of Culture and a Sense of History: A Feminist Critique of Cultural Essentialism," in *Decentering the Center,* ed. Sandra Harding and Uma Narayan (Bloomington: Indiana University Press, 2000), 83.

21. Desai, "Hearing Afghan Women's Voices," 841.

22. Ibid., 843.

23. Butler et al., *Contingency, Hegemony, Universality,* 35.

24. U.S. Congress, *Afghan People vs. the Taliban: The Struggle for Freedom Intensifies,* 107th Cong., 1st sess. (October 31, 2001).

25. An-Na'im, "State Responsibility Under International Human Rights Law to Change Religious and Customary Laws," in *The Human Rights of Women: National and International Perspectives*, ed. Rebecca J. Cook (Philadelphia: University of Pennsylvania Press, 1994), 174.

26. For example, Michelle McKinley, "Cultural Culprits," *Berkeley Journal of Gender, Law and Justice* 24, no. 2 (2009): 91–165; Nilda Rimonte, "A Question of Culture," *Stanford Law Review* 43, no. 6 (July 1991): 1311–26; Leti Volpp, "Talking 'Culture': Gender, Race, Nation and the Politics of Multiculturalism," *Columbia Law Review* 96 (October 1996): 1573.

27. Butler et al., *Contingency, Hegemony, Universality*.

28. Denise Ferreira da Silva, "Towards a Critique of the Socio-logos of Justice: The Analytics of Raciality and the Production of Universality," *Social Identities* 7, no. 3 (2001): 421–54.

29. See Denise Ferreira da Silva, *The Global Idea of Race* (Minneapolis: University of Minnesota Press, 2007), for work that traces the writing of modern man in Enlightenment and post-Enlightenment philosophical texts as well as in contemporary sociological literatures.

30. Ibid.

31. Jane Flax, *Thinking Fragments* (New York: Routledge, 1992), 447.

32. The legitimacy of governance was once simply ensured by the king's claim to God. One of the radical shifts in thinking that Enlightenment philosophers like John Locke set forth was to explain the legitimacy of governance that did not assume a ruler's claim to God. For Locke, the legitimacy of governance came from a social contract drawn out of man's mutual recognition for peace—a recognition that came from man's ability to reason.

33. Charlotte Bunch, "Taking Stock: Women's Human Rights Five Years after Beijing," in *Holding on to the Promise: Women's Human Rights and the Beijing +5 Review*, ed. Cynthia Meillon (New Brunswick: Rutgers University Press, 2001), 139.

34. Peter Fitzpatrick, *Mythology of Modern Law*, 6, 10.

35. Ibid.

36. All United Nations antitrafficking PSAs are available at http://www.unodc.org/unodc/en/human-trafficking/human-trafficking-public-service-announcements.html (accessed February 13, 2011) or at http://www.unodc.org/unodc/multimedia.html?vf=/documents/video/psa/HT_PSA_Telephone_2003.flv (accessed July 1, 2010). Thanks to Grace Kim for drawing my attention to the PSAs, specifically "Cleaning Woman" and "Telephone," which she viewed on AFN while in South Korea in 2003–4.

37. With Kasturi Ray, I provide a more detailed analysis of *Cleaning Woman* (previously named *Cleaning Lady*) in "The Practice of Humanity," *Feminist Media Studies* 10, no. 3 (2010): 253–67.

38. U.S. Congress, House of Representatives, Committee on International Relations, "Statement of the Honorable John R. Miller," *Combating Human Trafficking: Achieving Zero Tolerance*, 109th Cong., 1st sess. (March 9, 2005).

Available at http://commdocs.house.gov/committees/intlrel/hfa99820.000/
hfa99820_of.htm (accessed February 13, 2011).

39. U.S. Congress, House of Representatives, *Trafficking in Persons,* 109th
Cong., 2nd sess. (Washington, D.C.: Government Printing Office, 2007).

40. Cynthia Enloe, *Banana, Beaches and Bases* (Berkeley and Los Angeles:
University of California Press, 1990).

41. Meghana Nayak, "Interrogations of Democracy, Sexual Violence, and
the U.S. Military," in *Theorizing Sexual Violence,* ed. Renee Heberle and Victoria
Grace (New York: Routledge, 2009), 157.

42. In her work, Michelle McKinley traces how cultural culprits are constructed in U.S. asylum cases involving female genital cutting. She argues that
these cases demonstrate the way "invocation of 'culture' as a 'cracking factor'
or as a justification for criminal behavior in U.S. courtrooms reinforces an
already widely held assumption about the incommensurability of gender equality and non-western cultures," which works to frame arguments through a "sav-
ages–victims–saviors" triad. McKinley, "Cultural Culprits," *Berkeley Journal of
Gender, Law and Justice* 24, no. 2 (2009): 95.

2. Speaking Subjects, Classifying Consent

1. U.S. Congress, *International Trafficking in Persons: Taking Action to Elim-
inate Modern Day Slavery,* 110th Cong., 1st sess., 2007, S. No. 11-119, 46.

2. "(Eva Petrova's) Letter to U.S. Authorities Denying Human Trafficking Victimization," *Trakhtenberg,* No. 02-cr-00638, Exhibit A to 141 at 5 (New
Jersey filed July 6, 2005).

3. Judgment in a Criminal Case, *Trakhtenberg,* 145 at 5 (New York filed
June 20, 2005).

4. "(Eva Petrova's) Letter to U.S. Authorities Denying Human Trafficking
Victimization."

5. Jennifer Dunn, *Judging Victims* (Boulder, Colo.: Lynne Rienner Publishers, 2010), 4.

6. Charles Piot, "Representing Africa in the Kasinga Asylum Case," in
Female Circumcision: A Multicultural Perspective, ed. Rogaia Mustafa Abusharaf
(Philadelphia: University of Pennsylvania Press, 2006), 230.

7. See, for example, Mary Frances Berry, *The Pig Farmer's Daughter and
Other Tales of American Justice* (New York: Vintage, 1999); A. Cheree Carlson,
The Crimes of Womanhood: Defining Femininity in a Court of Law (Urbana: Univer-
sity of Illinois Press, 2009); Adrienne Davis, "The Private Law of Race and Sex,"
in *Mixed Race America and the Law,* ed. Kevin Johnson (New York: New York
University Press, 2003), 243–53.

8. Dina Francesca Haynes, "(Not) Found Chained to a Bed in a Brothel,"
Georgetown Immigration Law Journal 21, no. 3 (2007), available at http://papers
.ssrn.com/sol3/papers.cfm?abstract_id=984927 (accessed February 13, 2011).

9. See INCITE! Women of Color Against Violence, eds., *Color of Violence*
(Cambridge, Mass.: South End Press, 2006).

10. Catharine MacKinnon, *Sex Equality: Rape Law* (New York: Foundation Press, 2001), 801.

11. Ibid., 817.

12. Nicola Gavey, "Fighting Rape," in *Theorizing Sexual Violence*, ed. Renee Heberle and Victoria Grace (New York: Routledge, 2009), 111.

13. Susan Caringella, *Addressing Rape Reform in Law and Practice* (New York: Columbia University Press, 2009), 13–17.

14. MacKinnon, *Sex Equality*, 12; Meghana Nayak, "Interrogations of Democracy, Sexual Violence, and the U.S. Military," in *Theorizing Sexual Violence*, ed. Renee Heberle and Victoria Grace (New York: Routledge, 2009), 151.

15. Elizabeth Schneider, "Battered Women, Feminist Lawmaking, Privacy, and Equality," in *Women and the United States Constitution*, ed. Sibyl Schwarzenback and Patricia Smith (New York: Columbia University Press, 2003), 199, 201.

16. Mary Frances Berry chronicles many such instances, where the so-called private matters of married life were central to both civil and criminal court proceedings, in *The Pig Farmer's Daughter*.

17. Dorothy McBride Stetson, *Women's Rights in the USA: Policy Debates and Gender Roles* (New York: Garland, 1997), 310.

18. Janine Young Kim, "Racial Politics and Discretion in Criminal Law," in *Race to Injustice: Lessons Learned from the Duke Lacrosse Rape Case,* ed. Michael L. Seigel (Durham: Carolina Academic Press, 2009), 164.

19. Ibid., 160.

20. Aviva Orenstein, "Presuming Guilt or Protecting Victims? Analyzing the Special Treatment of Those Accused of Rape," in *Race to Injustice: Lessons Learned from the Duke Lacrosse Rape Case,* ed. Michael L. Seigel (Durham: Carolina Academic Press, 2009), 353.

21. Valerie Smith, *Not Just Race, Not Just Gender* (New York: Routledge, 1998), 5.

22. Ibid., 8.

23. Elizabeth Philipose, "Feminist, International Law, and the Spectacular Violence of the 'Other,'" in *Theorizing Sexual Violence*, ed. Renee Heberle and Victoria Grace (New York: Routledge, 2009), 177–78.

24. HR 3244, Section 103.2.

25. Ibid., 349.

26. Haynes, "(Not) Found Chained to a Bed in a Brothel," 351.

27. See Joanna Bourke, foreword to *Theorizing Sexual Violence*, ed. Renee Heberle and Victoria Grace (New York: Routledge, 2009), ix–xiii.

28. Sylvanna Falcon, "'National Security' and the Violation of Women," in *Color of Violence*, ed. INCITE! Women of Color Against Violence (Cambridge: South End Press, 2006), 119–37; Eithne Luibheid, *Entry Denied: Controlling Sexuality at the Border* (Minneapolis: University of Minnesota Press, 2002), 103–35.

29. Jo Doezema, "Loose Women or Lost Women? The Re-emergence of the Myth of White Slavery in Contemporary Discourses of Trafficking in Women," *Gender Issues* 18, no. 1 (2000): 23–50.

30. Martha Gardner, *Qualities of a Citizen* (Princeton: Princeton University Press, 2005).

31. Peggy Pascoe, *What Comes Naturally* (Oxford: Oxford University Press, 2009).

32. Gardner, *Qualities of a Citizen*, 60.

33. See, for example, Vidyamali Samarasinghe, *Female Sex Trafficking in Asia: The Resilience of Patriarchy in a Changing World* (New York: Routledge, 2008), 147–52; Felicity Schaeffer-Grabiel, "The Erotics of Citizenship: Cybermarriage, Marriage and the Virtual Imagination across the Americas" (University of California, Santa Cruz).

34. Luibheid, *Entry Denied*, 31–54.

35. Gardner, *Qualities of a Citizen*, 56, 60.

36. The various political, economic, and social shifts taking place at the turn of the twentieth century that helped extend the category of whiteness beyond its previous definition are explored in David Roediger's *Working toward Whiteness: How America's Immigrants Became White* (New York: Basic Books, 2005).

37. Gardner, *Qualities of a Citizen*, 60.

38. Wendy Chapkis, "Soft Glove, Punishing Fist," in *Regulating Sex: The Politics of Intimacy and Identity*, ed. Elizabeth Bernstein and Laurie Schaffner (New York: Routledge, 2004), 51–66; Gretchen Soderlund, "Running from the Rescuers: New U.S. Crusades against Sex Trafficking and the Rhetoric of Abolition," *NWSA Journal* 17, no. 3 (2005): 64–86; Kay Warren, "The 2000 U.N. Human Trafficking Protocol: Rights, Enforcement, Vulnerabilities," in *The Practice of Human Rights*, ed. Sally Engle Merry and Mark Goodale (Cambridge: Cambridge University Press, 2007), 242–69.

39. Janet Halley et al., "From the International to the Local in Feminist Legal Responses to Rape, Prostitution/Sex Work, and Sex Trafficking," *Harvard Journal of Law and Gender* 29 (Summer 2006): 336–419; H. Richard Friman and Simon Reich, "Human Trafficking and the Balkans," in *Human Trafficking, Human Security and the Balkans*, ed. Friman and Reich (Pittsburgh: University of Pittsburgh Press, 2007), 8.

40. Soderlund, "Running from the Rescuers."

41. Samarasinghe, *Female Sex Trafficking in Asia*, 4.

42. Julia O'Connell Davidson, "Will the Real Sex Slave Please Stand Up?" *Feminist Review* 83 (2006): 4–22.

43. Warren, "2000 U.N. Human Trafficking Protocol," 244, 247.

44. U.S. Department of State, "Identifying and Helping Trafficking Victims: Fact Sheet," available at http://www.state.gov/g/tip/c16508.htm (accessed October 1, 2007).

45. This figure is the application fee for filing for the T visa. Fees until 2008 were $270 plus a $70 biometric fee per applicant. The cost for dependents was $120 plus the $70 biometric fee. Under President Obama, the filing fee for the T visa was reduced to $0. Visa application, cost, and instructions can be accessed at http://www/uscis/gov/files/form/I-914.pdf.

46. Chapkis, "Soft Glove, Punishing Fist," 51–65; Davidson, "Will the Real Sex Slave Please Stand Up?," 4–22; Doezema, "Loose Women or Lost Women?," 23–50; Haynes, "(Not) Found Chained to a Bed in a Brothel," 337–81; Kamala Kempadoo, "Women of Color and the Global Sex Trade: Transnational Feminist Perspectives," *Meridians* 1, no. 2 (2001): 28–51.

47. Beverly Balos and Mary Lou Fellows, "A Matter of Prostitution: Becoming Respectable," *New York University Law Review* 74 (1999): 1220.

48. Luibheid, *Entry Denied*, 48.

49. Nandita Sharma, "Anti-Trafficking Rhetoric and the Making of Global Apartheid," *NWSA Journal* 17, no. 3 (2005): 88.

50. U.S. Department of Justice et al., "Assessment of U.S. Government Efforts to Combat Trafficking in Persons in Fiscal Year 2005" (Washington, D.C.: Government Printing Office, September 2006), 7, available at http://www.justice .gov/archive/ag/annualreports/tr2006/assessment_of_efforts_to_combat_tip .pdf (accessed February 13, 2011). In its first year, the program assisted five certified victims of trafficking in returning to the home countries. The number of family reunifications with victims remaining in the United States is higher; in the first year, the program aided thirty-three individuals.

51. Samarasinghe, *Female Sex Trafficking in Asia.*

52. Ratha Kapur, "Legal Politics and Anti-Trafficking Interventions," in *Trafficking in Humans,* ed. Sally Cameron and Edward Newman (New York: United Nations University Press, 2008), 113.

53. Kinsey Dinan, "Globalization and National Sovereignty," in *Trafficking in Humans,* ed. Sally Cameron and Edward Newman (New York: United Nations University Press, 2008), 75.

54. Deborah Mindry, "Nongovernmental Organization, 'Grassroots,' and the Politics of Virtue," *Signs* 26, no. 4 (2001): 1193.

55. Charles Briggs, "Mediating Infanticide: Theorizing Relations between Narrative and Violence," *Cultural Anthropology* 22, no. 3 (2007): 315–56.

56. Superseding Indictment, *Rosales-Martinez,* 19 at 14–15 (New Jersey filed July 21, 2005). Other trafficking case taking place in 2005 where women are documented as having forced abortions include *United States v. Carreto* (No. 04-cr-00140, 71 at 5 [E.D. New York filed March 3, 2005]) and *United States v. Salazar* (No. 05-cr-00371, 1 at 6, filed August 1, 2005).

57. See Soderlund, "Running from the Rescuers."

58. *United States v. Babaev,* No. 05-cr-00500, 8 at 4 (ED New York filed November 30, 2005).

59. Luibheid, *Entry Denied*, 47.

60. Warren, "2000 U.N. Human Trafficking Protocol," 247.

61. Kapur, "Legal Politics of Anti-Trafficking Interventions," 119.

62. Michelle McKinley, "Cultural Culprits," *Berkeley Journal of Gender, Law and Justice* 24, no. 2 (2009): 114–15.

63. Saba Mahmood, *Politics of Piety* (Princeton: Princeton University Press, 2005), 18.

64. McKinley, "Cultural Culprits," 116.

65. U.S. Department of State, *Trafficking in Persons Report* (Washington, D.C.: Government Printing Office, June 2007), 37, available at http://www.state.gov/g/tip/rls/tiprpt/2007/ (accessed February 13, 2011).

66. Gayatri Chakravorty Spivak, "Can the Subaltern Speak?," in *Marxism and the Interpretation of Culture,* ed. Cary Nelson and Lawrence Grossberg (Urbana: University of Illinois Press, 1988), 279.

67. Joan Scot, "The Evidence of Experience," *Critical Inquiry* 17 (Summer 1991): 773–97.

68. Ibid., 778.

69. Ien Ang, "I'm a Feminist But . . . 'Other' Women and Postnational Feminism," in *Feminism and "Race,"* ed. Kum-Kum Bhavnani (New York: Oxford University Press, 2001), 396.

70. Judith Butler, *Bodies That Matter: On the Discursive Limits of "Sex"* (New York: Routledge, 1993), 220.

71. Avery Gordon, *Ghostly Matters* (Minneapolis: University of Minnesota Press, 1997), 4.

3. Front-Page News

1. Charles Briggs, "Mediating Infanticide: Theorizing Relations between Narrative and Violence," *Cultural Anthropology* 22, no. 3 (2007): 323, 324.

2. Gretchen Soderlund, "Running from the Rescuers: New U.S. Crusades against Sex Trafficking and the Rhetoric of Abolition," *NWSA Journal* 17, no. 3 (Fall 2005): 69.

3. Landesman, "The Girls Next Door," *New York Times,* January 25, 2004, available at http://query.nytimes.com/gst/fullpage.html?res=9B04EEDA1439 F936A15752C0A9629C8B63 (accessed February 13, 2011).

4. Gaye Tuchman, *Making News: A Study of the Construction of Reality* (New York: Free Press, 1978), 3.

5. In the *MSNBC Undercover* special "Sex Slaves in America," for instance, the program chronicles three stories of sex trafficking, one featuring Eastern Europe, the second Latin America, and the third Asia. A key early report on trafficking researched in 1999 by an analyst with the State Department's Bureau of Intelligence and Research, Center for the Study of Intelligence, states that "the primary source countries" for human trafficking activities include "Thailand, Vietnam, China, Mexico, Russia, Ukraine and the Czech Republic. Women have also been trafficked to the U.S. from the Philippines, Korea, Malaysia, Latvia, Hungary, Poland, Brazil and Honduras among other countries." Subsequent state documents, including the annual State Department publication *Trafficking in Persons Reports,* Government Accountability Office reports, and Congressional Research Service reports, have reiterated this information, noting that most women who find themselves victim to trafficking in the United States are nonnationals. Amy O'Neill Richard, *International Trafficking in Women to the United States: A Contemporary Manifestation of Slavery and Organized Crime,* Center for the Study of Intelligence (Washington, D.C.: Government Printing

Office, April 2000), 3, available at https://www.cia.gov/library/center-for-the-study-of-intelligence/csi-publications/books-and-monographs/trafficking
.pdf (accessed June 25, 2010).

6. "Teen Girls' Stories of Sex Trafficking in U.S.," *ABC News* (February 9, 2006), http://abcnews.go.com/print?id=1596778 (accessed July 11, 2007); Nicholas Kristof, "A Heroine from the Brothels," *New York Times*, September 25, 2008, available at http://www.nytimes.com/2008/09/25/opinion/25kristof
.html (accessed February 13, 2011).

7. Other news media features (either televised specials, books, or lengthy newspaper series in papers with national circulation) include *MSNBC Under-cover*'s special, "Sex Slaves in America," as reported by Meredith Viera (December 3, 2007); a *Dateline* special on Cambodia's sex industry, "Children for Sale"; Nicholas Kristof's op-ed series on sex trafficking for the *New York Times;* Canadian journalist Victor Malarek's *The Natashas;* Scottish journalist Craig McGill's *Human Traffic;* and the *New York Review*'s "Women and Children for Sale," by Caroline Moorehead.

8. Briggs, "Mediating Infanticide," 331.

9. "Sex Slaves" (transcript), *Frontline* (PBS), written and directed by Ric Esther Bienstock, 2005, available at http://www.pbs.org/wgbh/pages/frontline/slaves/etc/script.html (accessed November 21, 2007).

10. Ric Esther Bienstock notes in an interview, "It is my hope that the film will inspire people to do something about this [sex trafficking]. We have also set up a trust fund so that we can direct some money to the victims who shared their stories with us." *Frontline* interview with Ric Esther Bienstock, "Director's Notes," http://www.pbs.org/wgbh/pages/frontline/slaves/making/ (accessed November 21, 2007).

11. See, for instance, Mark Pedelty, *War Stories: The Culture of Foreign Corre-spondents* (New York: Routledge, 1995). Pedelty's chapter, "The Narrative Structure and Agenda of Objective Journalism," notes that "emotional concern is anathema to objective journalism" where the guise of writing objectively is instituted through eliminating any explicit reference to values, politics, or emotion (170).

12. *Frontline* interview with Ric Esther Bienstock, "Director's Notes."

13. Pedelty, *War Stories*, 181.

14. Colin Sparks notes in "The Panic over Tabloid News," in *Tabloid Tales: Global Debates over Media Standards,* ed. Colin Sparks and John Tulloch (New York: Rowman and Littlefield, 2000), 1–40, that definitions of what constitutes tabloid news are not clear-cut. While "in the United States 'tabloidization' is seen as something coming from outside the world of proper, respectable journalism," the distinction between respectable journalism and tabloids cannot be understood "in terms of a simple binary opposition" (7, 13).

15. Daniel Hallin and Paolo Mancini, *Comparing Media Systems* (New York: Cambridge University Press, 2004), 198.

16. For instance, Sparks and Tulloch, *Tabloid Tales,* and Stephen Bloom,

Inside the Writer's Mind: Writing Narrative Journalism (Ames: Iowa State University Press, 2002), both of which describe the rise of first-person journalism in the United States, although Bloom also notes that first-personal journalism "isn't an excuse for personal indulgence" (viii). Although first-person journalism is part of serious news outlets and objectivity is itself a myth, there is still a writing and narrative convention in such sites that privileges the idea of neutral, value-free, and emotion-free reporting. See also Tuchman, *Making News.*

17. Siddharth Kara, *Sex Trafficking* (New York: Columbia University Press, 2009), 98.

18. Columbia University Press, "Siddharth Kara, Author of *Sex Trafficking*," YouTube video, available at http://www.youtube.com/watch?v=QOGf5ml39kA (accessed June 10, 2010).

19. Julie Bindel, "Press for Change: Guide for Journalists Reporting on the Prostitution and Trafficking of Women" (Coalition Against Trafficking in Women, 2006), available at http://action.web.ca/home/catw/readingroom .shtml?x=93526&AA_EX_Session=c22c71d6ffd97deeb9380562b3162f77 (accessed February 13, 2011), 26.

20. An ethical john is part of the *MSNBC Undercover* program "Sex Slaves in America." One of the victims whom the story features, Katya, escapes from her conditions through a customer who promises to help her and her friend. Transcripts of the program are available at http://www.msnbc.com/id/220 56066/ (accessed December 6, 2007).

21. Meredith May, "Diary of a Sex Slave: Free, but Trapped," *San Francisco Chronicle*, October 10, 2006, A8.

22. Meredith May, "Diary of a Sex Slave: Life in LA," *San Francisco Chronicle*, October 9, 2006, A7.

23. May, "Diary of a Sex Slave: Free, but Trapped," A8.

24. Ibid.

25. Briggs, "Mediating Infanticide," 331.

26. See Joan Scott, "Evidence of Experience," *Critical Inquiry* 17, no. 4 (Summer 1991): 773–97.

27. As described by Bindel, "Press for Change."

28. In Malarek's *The Natashas* (New York: Arcade Publishing, 2004), 234–38, it is his intervention that helps expose corruption within DynCorp, a private company hiring U.S. police to serve in U.N. missions in places like Bosnia-Herzegovina. When the police raid to bust a trafficking ring is called off for unknown and suspicious reasons, it is Malarek, not the U.N. police officer in charge of leading the raid whom Malarek shadows, who exposes the incompetence and implied corruption of a DynCorp employee, John Randolph.

29. Bindel, "Press for Change," 25.

30. United States Department of State, Office to Monitor and Combat Trafficking in Persons, *Trafficking in Persons Report* (June 2007), 10, available at http://www.state.gov/g/tip/rls/tiprpt/2007/ (accessed June 20, 2010).

31. Meredith May, "Diary of a Sex Slave: A Youthful Mistake," *San Francisco Chronicle*, October 8, A9.

32. Ibid., A7.

33. Ibid.

34. Ibid., A9.

35. United States Department of State, Office to Monitor and Combat Trafficking in Persons, *Trafficking in Persons Report* (June 11, 2003), available at http://www.state.gov/g/tip/rls/tiprpt/2003/ (accessed February 13, 2011).

36. May, "Dairy of a Sex Slave: A Youthful Mistake," A7.

37. Max Weber, *The Protestant Ethic and the Spirit of Capitalism* (Los Angeles: Roxbury Publishing, 1998), 57.

38. Ibid., 21.

39. May, "Dairy of a Sex Slave: A Youthful Mistake," A7.

40. Ibid., A9.

41. Donna M. Hughes, *Trafficking for Sexual Exploitation: The Case of the Russian Federation,* prepared for International Organization for Migration (Geneva, International Organization for Migration, 2002), 7.

42. For instance, Alyson Brody, Mantana Veerachai, Sarah Johnston, Siriporn Skrobanek, and Vachararutai Boontinand, *Trafficking in Women in the Asia-Pacific Region: A Regional Report* (Bangkok: Global Alliance Against Trafficking in Women [GAATW], 1997); Louise Brown, *Sex Slaves: The Trafficking of Women in Asia* (London: Virago Press, 2000); Leviseda Douglas, "Sex Trafficking in Cambodia," working paper 122 (Victoria, Australia: Center of Southeast Asian Studies, 2003); Patricia H. Hynes and Janice G. Raymond, "Put in Harm's Way: The Neglected Health Consequences of Sex Trafficking in the United States," in *Policing the National Body: Sex, Race, and Criminalization,* ed. Jael Silliman and Anannya Bhattacharjee (Cambridge: South End Press, 2002), 197–225; Siriporn Skrobanek, Nataya Boonpakdee, and Chutima Jantateero, *The Traffic in Women: Human Realities of the International Sex Trade* (New York: Zed Books, 1997).

43. May, "Diary of a Sex Slave: A Youthful Mistake," A7.

44. As noted in the 2007 *Trafficking in Persons Report,* the Department of States argues that "the globalization of markets and labor forces, and the concomitant relaxation of travel barriers have spawned new trafficking scenarios and routes."

45. Richard Thomas Ford, *Racial Culture: A Critique* (Princeton: Princeton University Press, 2005), 37.

46. Asian Watch, *A Modern Form of Slavery: Trafficking of Burmese Women and Girls into Brothels in Thailand* (New York: Human Rights Watch, 1993), 47.

47. Brown, *Sex Slaves,* 209.

48. In fact, Gary Haugen, president of the Christian nongovernmental organization International Rescue Mission, perhaps most vividly captures the writing of sex trafficking through the narrative of rescue, as Gretchen Soderlund has pointed out in "Running from the Rescuers."

49. Department of State, Office to Monitor and Combat Trafficking, *Trafficking in Persons Report* (June 2007), available at http://www.state.gov/g/tip/rls/tiprpt/2007/ (accessed February 13, 2011).

50. For example, Ann Veneman, executive director of UNICEF, noted at

the "United Front for Children: Global Efforts to Combat Sexual Trafficking in Travel and Tourism" (a conference on trafficking that operated under the banner of private-public partnership): "A Bangladeshi woman who was forced into prostitution in India at the age of 10, who was abused and impregnated . . . said, 'My dream is that my daughter does not have the same misfortune that I have had and that both of my children will go to school. Had I been educated, I would not have been in this state.' . . . Education is absolutely key, in my view, to addressing poverty, to addressing trafficking, to addressing so many of the issues that the developing world is confronting today. . . . Some of the world that has to be done is to reeducate the family itself, to create an acceptance and understanding it is ok on the part of the child and the family to come back together." The focus on education and Veneman's evocation of the victim narrative assumes that those like the Bangladeshi woman and her daughter would not find themselves trafficked into the sex industry if they are educated on (liberal) feminist values of self-awareness and gender equality. Not only is education key to addressing cultural attitudes around gender that lead women like the Bangladeshi woman into prostitution, but it is also a key component to combating poverty. Ann Veneman, "United Front for Children: Global Efforts to Combat Sexual Trafficking in Travel and Tourism" (transcript), Conference held at the University of Minnesota, Minneapolis, April 21–22, 2006. Thanks to Barbara Frey and the Human Rights Center at the University of Minnesota for hosting, sponsoring, and providing transcripts of the event.

51. Journalists, NGO, and U.S. governmental documents describe traffickers (primary victimizers) as always already criminal, usually noting how these men are already members of international criminal syndicates like the Japanese Yakuza, Chinese Triad, and Russian Mafia. See Kathryn Farr, *Sex Trafficking* (New York: Worth Publishers, 2005), 59; Craig McGill, *Human Traffic: Sex, Slaves and Immigration* (London: Vision Paperbacks, 2003); Francis T. Miko, *Trafficking in Persons: The U.S. and International Response CRS Report for Congress* (Washington, D.C.: Congressional Research Service, 2006), 3.

52. Dipesh Chakrabarty, *Provincializing Europe: Postcolonial Thought and Historical Difference* (Princeton: Princeton University Press, 2000), 8.

53. Denise Ferriera da Silva, *The Global Idea of Race* (Minneapolis: University of Minnesota Press, 2007).

54. May, "Diary of a Sex Slave: Free, but Trapped," A6.

55. "Sex Slaves" (transcript), *Frontline*.

56. Brown, *Sex Slaves*, 25.

57. Skrobanek, Boonpakdee, and Jantateero, *Traffic in Women*, viii.

58. Michelle McKinley, "Cultural Culprits," *Berkeley Journal of Gender, Law and Justice* 24, no. 2 (2009): 114.

59. Briggs, "Mediating Infanticide," 328.

60. Ibid., 331.

61. "New York Times Columnist Biography: Nicholas Kristof," *New York Times,* available at http://www.nytimes.com/ref/opinion/KRISTOF-BIO.html (accessed April 7, 2008).

62. Nicholas Kristof, "Girls for Sale," *New York Times*, January 17, 2004, available at http://www.nytimes.com/2004/01/17/opinion/girls-for-sale.html (accessed February 13, 2011).

63. Kristof, "Loss of Innocence," *New York Times*, January 28, 2004, available at http://www.nytimes.com/2004/01/28/opinion/loss-of-innocence.html (accessed February 13, 2011).

64. Ibid.

65. Tuchman, *Making News*, 215.

4. Seeing Race and Sexuality

1. Francis T. Miko, Congressional Research Service, "Trafficking in Persons: The U.S. and International Response" (Washington, D.C.: Library of Congress, January 19, 2006).

2. Jillian Sandell, "Transnational Ways of Looking" (San Francisco State University). In her work, Sandell discusses the ways a transnational register informs cultural apprehension of visual imagery in the twenty-first century. See also Sandell, "Transnational Ways of Seeing: Sexual and National Belonging in *Hedwig and the Angry Inch*," *Gender, Place and Culture: A Journal of Feminist Geography* 17, no. 2 (April 2010): 231–47.

3. Denise Ferreira da Silva, *Toward a Global Idea of Race* (Minneapolis: University of Minnesota Press, 2007), 29.

4. All campaign posters are available for download on the DHHS Web page, available at http://www.acf.hhs.gov/trafficking/about/posters.html (accessed February 13, 2011).

5. Mae Ngai, *Impossible Subjects: Illegal Aliens and the Making of Modern America* (Princeton: Princeton University Press, 2004), 8.

6. Lisa Lowe, *Immigrant Acts: On Asian American Cultural Politics* (Durham: Duke University Press, 1999), 4.

7. Yen Le Espiritu, *Asian American Women and Men* (Walnut Creek: AltaMira Press, 2000), 93.

8. Virginia Act to Preserve Racial Integrity, section 5 (1924), available at http://www2.vcdh.virginia.edu/encounter/projects/monacans/Contemporary_Monacans/racial.html (accessed July 10, 2010).

9. Mary Frances Berry, *The Pig Farmer's Daughter and Other Tales of American Justice* (New York: Vintage, 1999).

10. Angela Davis, *Women, Race, Class* (New York: Vintage, 1983).

11. For example, Tomas Almaguer, *Racial Fault Lines* (Berkeley and Los Angeles: University of California Press, 1994), demonstrates the relational construction of racial categories in the context of turn-of-the-century California.

12. "Images of Human Trafficking" Web page, available at http://www.gtipphotos.state.gov/ (accessed May 1, 2010).

13. Kay Chernush for the U.S. State Department, "Sexual Trafficking." http://www.gtipphotos.state.gov/.

14. The contrastive nature of the images is replicated in the 2007 *Trafficking in Persons* Report images. The photographs in the 2007 report featuring white European women include a head shot of Mara, a woman victim to sex trafficking, a photo similar to Chernush's Western Europe prostitution image in its blurry ambiguity with informative caption, and a reproduction of a Danish advertisement featuring a black-and-white head shot of a young, white female model. These are the only images in the report that reference white victims. The eight photos depicting sex trafficking and Asia present women in the act of negotiating with johns, scantily clad women, and group photos similar to the final image in Chernush's gallery.

15. Espiritu, *Asian American Women and Men*, 95.

16. Laura Kang, *Compositional Subjects: Enfiguring Asian/American Women* (Durham: Duke University Press, 2002), 93–94.

17. See Gina Marchetti, *Romance and the Yellow Peril* (Berkeley and Los Angeles: University of California Press, 1994), and Robert Lee, *Orientals* (Philadelphia: Temple University Press, 1999), for a discussion of the ways representations of Asian and Asian American women with white men in popular culture worked in particular historical and political contexts to "manage" U.S. race relations.

18. Kang, *Compositional Subjects*, 94.

19. These trends are evident in other state documents, including the 2007 Department of State *Trafficking in Persons* (TIP) Report. While the 2007 TIP Report notes that "most uncaptioned photographs in the Report are not images of confirmed trafficking victims, but are provided to show the myriad forms of exploitation that help define trafficking and the variety of cultures in which trafficking victims are found," the images that accompany the report nonetheless help to create a visual reference for sex trafficking and its victims. U.S. Department of State, *Trafficking in Persons Report* (2007), available at http://www.state.gov/g/tip/rls/tiprpt/2007/index.htm (accessed June 20, 2010).

20. See Neda Atanasoski, "Afterimages of Empire" (manuscript, University of California, Santa Cruz).

21. Victor Malarek, *The Natashas* (New York: Arcade Publishing, 2004), 5–6.

22. Ann Marie Bertone, "Sexual Trafficking in Women: International Political Economy and the Politics of Sex," *Gender Issues* 18, no. 1 (2000): 8.

23. Miko, "Trafficking in Persons," 2.

24. U.S. Congress, House of Representatives, *The Sex Trade: Trafficking of Women and Children in Europe and the United States*, 106th Cong., 1st sess. (June 28, 1999), 2.

25. Donna Hughes, *Trafficking for Sexual Exploitation: The Case of the Russian Federation* (Geneva: International Organization for Migration, June 2002).

26. Ibid., 7.

27. Elaine Brown, *The Ties That Bind: Migration and Trafficking of Women and Girls for Sexual Exploitation in Cambodia* (Geneva: International Organization for Migration, 2007), 7–8, available at http://www.humantrafficking.org/uploads/publications/IOM_trafficking_report_Aug07.pdf (accessed February 13, 2011).

28. Siddharth Kara, *Sex Trafficking: Inside the Business of Modern Slavery* (New York: Columbia University Press, 2009), 175.

29. Jodi Kim, *Ends of Empire: Asian American Critique and the Cold War* (Minneapolis: University of Minnesota Press, 2010), 37–93.

30. Samuel Huntington, "The Clash of Civilizations?" *Foreign Affairs* (Summer 1993): 49.

31. For instance, Lee, in *Orientals,* argues that Huntington's views posit that "America is threatened by the demand of non-European Americans for racial equality and social recognition" (207). For Lee, Huntington presents a worldview of "essentialized cultural difference" that "defines Asian Americans as inauthentic and the potential agents of a dreaded de-Westernization of American society" (208).

32. The PSA *Work Abroad* is available for download at http://www.unodc .org/unodc/multimedia.html?vf=/documents/video/psa/HT_PSA_Work_A broad_2001_60sec.flv (accessed February 13, 2011).

33. The other PSAs dealing with human trafficking produced during the early 2000s include *Cleaning Woman* (1998, 2003), *Better Future* (2002), and *Telephone* (2003). All PSAs are available at http://www.unodc.org/unodc/en/ multimedia.html (accessed February 13, 2011).

34. Ambassador John Miller, senior advisor for the Secretary of State on Human Trafficking, at the "United Front for Children: Global Efforts to Combat Sexual Trafficking in Travel and Tourism" conference, April 21–22, 2006, University of Minnesota.

35. Max Weber, *The Protestant Ethic and the Spirit of Capitalism* (Los Angeles: Roxbury Publishing, 1998), 26.

36. Ironically, even though China and Vietnam persist in the literature as hot spots for trafficking, the role of the communist state only appears in terms of government failures to combat trafficking, and cultural explanations remain central. For example, in a congressional hearing on trafficking in China held in 2006, Steven Law, deputy secretary of the U.S. Department of Labor, points out that cultural factors (in addition to migration, poverty, and proximity to other nations where trafficking is pervasive) such as "forced marriage and the unique pressures created by the Chinese Governments' one child policy" contribute to trafficking in China. U.S. Congress, *Combating Human Trafficking in China: Domestic and International Efforts,* 109th Cong., 2nd sess. (March 6, 2006), 5, available at http://www.cecc.gov (accessed May 1, 2010).

37. Hughes, *Trafficking for Sexual Exploitation,* 7.

38. Lucinda Peach, "Buddhism and Human Rights in the Thai Sex Trade," in *Religious Fundamentalisms and the Human Rights of Women,* ed. Courtney Howland (New York: Palgrave, 1999), 215, 221.

39. Hughes, *Trafficking for Sexual Exploitation,* 13.

40. As a Coalition Against Trafficking in Women (CATW) report notes, a key factor to promoting sex trafficking includes "macro-economic policies . . . that mandate 'structural adjustments' in many developing regions of the world, pushing certain countries (e.g. the Philippines) to export women for labor,

making them vulnerable to trafficking; or to develop economies based on tourism (e.g. Thailand)." Janice Raymond, Donna Hughes, and Carol Gomez, "Sex Trafficking of Women in the United States," Coalition Against Trafficking in Women, March 2001, available at http://www.uri.edu/artsci/wms/hughes/sex_traff_us.pdf (accessed February 13, 2011), 17.

5. Refiguring Slavery

1. Tani Barlow, "International Feminism of the Future," *Signs* 25, no. 4 (2000): 1101.

2. Nikhil Pal Singh, *Black Is a Country* (Cambridge: Harvard University Press, 2004), 4.

3. Ibid., 10.

4. Deborah Cohler, "Keeping the Home Front Burning: Renegotiating Gender and Sexuality in U.S. Mass Media after September 11," *Feminist Media Studies* 6, no. 3 (2006): 245.

5. Denise Ferreira da Silva, *Toward a Global Idea of Race* (Minneapolis: University of Minnesota Press, 2007).

6. Singh, *Black Is a Country,* 4, 33.

7. Silva, *Toward a Global Idea of Race,* xxx.

8. Polaris Project Web site, available at http://www.polarisproject.org/about-us/introduction (accessed February 13, 2011).

9. President George W. Bush, "President Bush Addresses United Nations General Assembly," United Nations, New York, September 23, 2003, available at http://www.whitehouse.gov/news/releases/2003/09/print/20030923-4.html (accessed September 26, 2004).

10. Free the Slaves is a nongovernmental organization that describes its mission as one "to end slavery worldwide" (http://www.freetheslaves.net; accessed February 13, 2011). Kevin Bales, *Understanding Global Slavery* (Berkeley and Los Angeles: University of California Press, 2005).

11. John Miller, "Orange Grove: Slavery Alive and Well in the U.S.," *Orange County Register,* November 15, 2006.

12. U.S. Congress, Committee on the Judiciary, Subcomittee on the Constitution, Civil Rights and Property Rights, "Examining U.S. Efforts to Combat Human Trafficking and Slavery," 108th Cong., 2nd sess. (July 7, 2004).

13. A. Leon Higginbotham Jr., *Shades of Freedom: Racial Politics and the Presumptions of the American Legal Process* (New York: Oxford University Press, 1996).

14. George Lipsitz, *The Possessive Investment in Whiteness: How White People Profit from Identity Politics* (Philadelphia: Temple University Press, 2006).

15. Singh, *Black Is a Country.*

16. Gretchen Soderlund, "Running from the Rescuers: New U.S. Crusades against Sex Trafficking and the Rhetoric of Abolition," *NWSA Journal* 17, no. 3 (Fall 2005): 76. Soderlund discusses the example of Venezuela in 2004, when it, along with Cuba and North Korea, was one of only ten nations categorized as tier 3 (the lowest ranking).

17. Ibid., 67.

18. Maylei Blackwell and Nadine Naber, "Intersectionality in an Era of Globalization," *Merdians* 2, no. 2 (2002): 239.

19. Bush, "President Bush Addresses United Nations General Assembly."

20. Kathryn Sikkink, *Mixed Signals* (Ithaca: Cornell University Press, 2004), 5.

21. John Locke, "Of the State of Nature," *Second Treatise of Government* (Cambridge: Hackett Publishing, 1980), 9.

22. Ibid., 8.

23. Laura Bush, "President, Mrs. Bush Mark Progress in Global Women's Human Rights," remarks given on March 12, 2004, available at http://white house.gov/news/releases/2004/03/pring/20040312-5.html (accessed September 26, 2004).

24. Cohler, "Keeping the Home Front Burning," 245–46.

25. Joan Scott, "Universalism and the History of Feminism," *Differences* 7, no. 1 (1995): 3.

26. Cohler, "Keeping the Home Front Burning," 246.

27. U.S. Congress, House of Representatives, *Trafficking of Women and Children in the International Sex Trade*, 106th Cong., 1st sess. (September 14, 1999), 40.

28. Rice, "Remarks at the White House Conference on the Americas," Hyatt Regency Hotel, Crystal City, Va., July 9, 2007, available at http://www.state.gov/secretary/rm/2007/87996.htm (accessed April 14, 2008).

29. Singh, *Black Is a Country.*

30. Silva, *Toward a Global Idea of Race*, 201.

31. Reginald Horsman, *Race and Manifest Destiny* (Cambridge: Harvard University Press, 1981).

32. Silva, *Toward a Global Idea of Race*, 204.

33. Ibid., xv.

34. Henry Yu, *Thinking Orientals: Migration, Contact and Exoticism in Modern America* (New York: Oxford University Press, 2001), 45.

35. Ibid., 62.

36. Lisa Lowe, *Immigrant Acts* (Durham: Duke University Press, 1996), 86.

37. David Hollinger, *Postethnic America: Beyond Multiculturalism* (New York: HarperCollins, 1995), 129.

38. Singh, *Black Is a Country*, 17.

39. Ibid., 17.

40. Ien Ang, "I'm a Feminist But . . . ," in *Feminism and Race*, ed. Kum-Kum Bhavnani (New York: Oxford University Press, 2001), 403.

41. Rachel Lee, "Notes from the (Non)Field," *Meridians* 1, no. 1 (2000): 86.

42. Judith Butler, *Gender Trouble* (New York: Routledge, 1999), 4.

43. For example, Kimberle Crenshaw, bell hooks, Valerie Smith, and Elizabeth Spelman.

44. Lee, "Notes from a (Non)Field," 91.

45. See, for instance, Alys Wienbaum, *Wayward Reproductions* (Durham: Duke University Press, 2004); Peggy Pascoe, *What Comes Naturally* (New York: Oxford University Press, 2009).

46. Valerie Smith, *Not Just Race, Not Just Gender: Black Feminist Readings* (New York: Routledge, 1998), xv.

47. The definition of trafficking provided in the 2000 United Nations Protocol to Prevent, Suppress and Punish Trafficking in Persons differs from the definition in the VTVPA over the matter of consent of victims. According to the protocol, "The consent of a victim of trafficking in persons to the intended exploitation set forth . . . shall be irrelevant." Rather, the protocol focuses on the presence of exploitation.

48. M. Jacqui Alexander and Chandra Talpade Mohanty, "Genealogies, Legacies, Movements," in *Feminism and Race,* ed. Kum-Kum Bhavnani (New York: Oxford University Press, 2001), 492.

49. U.S. Congress, House of Representatives, *Trafficking of Women and Children in the International Sex Trade,* 106th Cong., 1st sess. (September 14, 1999), 40.

50. Free the Slaves, "How You Can Help," available at http://www.freethelsaves.net (accessed February 13, 2011).

51. Nicholas Kristof, "Stopping the Traffickers," *New York Times,* January 31, 2004.

52. Emancipation Network, "Help Us Help Survivors: Made by Survivors," available at http://www.madebysurvivors.com/ (accessed February 13, 2011).

53. Ibid.

54. Emancipation Network, "About Us: How We Became Abolitionists Fighting Slavery, Sex Trafficking, and Human Trafficking," available at http://www.madebysurvivors.com/FoundersStory (accessed February 13, 2011).

55. Nicole Yorio, "Rescuing Girls and Women from the Sex Trade," *Redbook Magazine,* June 2010, 120–23.

56. U.S. Department of State, *Trafficking in Persons Report,* Publication 11407 (June 2009), 24, available at http://www.state.gov/g/tip (accessed February 13, 2011).

Conclusion

1. Sangtin Writers and Richa Nagar, *Playing with Fire* (Minneapolis: University of Minnesota Press, 2006), xxviii.

2. Inderpal Grewal and Caren Kaplan, "Transnational Feminist Practices and Questions of Postmodernity," in *Scattered Hegemonies: Postmodernity and Transnational Feminist Practices,* ed. Inderpal Grewal and Caren Kaplan (Minneapolis: University of Minnesota Press, 1994), 17.

3. Jacqueline Bhabha, "Embodied Rights: Gender Persecution, State Sovereignty and Refugees," in *Women, Citizenship and Difference,* ed. Nira Yuval-Davis and Prina Werbner (New York: Zed Books, 1999), 178.

4. Sally Engle Merry, *Human Rights and Gender Violence: Translating International Law into Local Justice* (Chicago: University of Chicago Press, 2006).

Index

Africa, xviii, 35, 114
African American. *See* black
agency, xiv–xv, 44–47, 66–67, 90,
   125; and negotiation, 45, 46;
   and self–determination, 63–65,
   89, 91–93, 104; and self–speech,
   46–48; agent, as subject, 28, 67,
   89, 94
Agustin, Laura Maria, xv
Alexander, Jacqui, xxiv, 113–14
Ali, Hirsi, 114
American Anthropological Association, 3, 4
American Dream, xxvi–xxvii, 50, 58,
   59, 107, 113
An-Na'im, Abdullahi Ahmcd, 15
Asia: as geographical location, xviii,
   64, 68, 71, 77, 78, 108, 114; as
   racialized difference, xxvii, 35–37,
   63, 64, 73, 75, 79, 80, 82–83, 85–
   86, 108; and perceived patriarchy,
   81, 82, 84–85, 90, 92; perception
   of sex trafficking origins, 63, 82–
   86, 87, 89, 90–92; regulation of
   sexuality, 36–38, 75, 90
Asian American, 23, 73, 80, 113
assimilation, xxiii–xxiv, 108, 110–11
asylum, 10–11, 123

Bales, Kevin, 97
Balos, Beverly, xv
being: onto-epistemology, xxix, 2,
   93, 111; ontology, xiv, xv–xvi, xxiv,
   xxv, 67, 72; ways of being, xiv, xv–
   xvi, xxix, 7, 67
Bertone, Andrea, 82–83

"Better Future," 21. *See also* United
   Nations, public service
   announcements
Bhabha, Jacqueline, 123
Bienstock, Ric Esther. *See* PBS *Front-
   line*, "Sex Slaves"
black, 10, 32–33, 35, 86, 98, 99,
   106, 107, 109–15
Boaz, Franz, 3
Briggs, Charles, 49–50
Brownmiller, Susan, 32
Bunch, Charlotte, 8, 19
Bush, George W., xix, 23, 97, 99–100,
   105; administration, 38, 39, 101–2
Bush, Laura, 103–5

Chapkis, Wendy, xv, 40
Charlesworth, Hillary, 8
Charvet, John, xxiii
choice, xiv–xv, 25, 45, 47, 63–64,
   66–69, 89, 95, 121–22. *See also*
   consent
citizenship, xx, xxi, 30, 41, 72, 73,
   75, 105, 110–11, 117, 118, 119,
   125; and national belonging, 71,
   73, 75, 80, 110–11; citizenry, xxi,
   5, 39, 42; policing of, xxi, 29, 35–
   37, 39, 75–76. *See also* nation
civil rights, xxiii–xxiv, xxviii; era,
   xxiii–xxiv, 80, 98–99, 111; post–
   civil rights, xxiii, 99
"Cleaning Woman," 21, 22–23, 24.
   See also United Nations, public
   service announcements
Clinton, Bill, xvii; administration,
   83–84

Julietta Hua is assistant professor of women and gender studies at San Francisco State University.